History of Sport

For Amy

History of Sport:

A Guide to the Literature and Sources of Information

Richard William Cox

British Society of Sport History
in association with
Sports History Publishing

Copyright © Richard William Cox 1994

Published by The British Society of Sport History
in association with Sports History Publishing
13 Bradley Lane, Frodsham, Cheshire WA6 6QA

British Library cataloguing in publication data
Cox, Richard (Richard William)
    History of Sport: A Guide to the Literature
    Sources of Information

ISBN 1 898010 03 X

Printed in Great Britain by Antony Rowe Ltd. Chippenham

Contents

Foreword

by Mr D. J. Foskett O.B.E., M.A., F.L.A., Formerly Librarian, University of London

The serious study of sports history has a relatively short history itself, but shows all the characteristics of scholarly investigation. It impinges on many aspects of life, social, technological, even psychological, as well as descriptions of current events, and it illustrates the growing importance of sport as a worthwhile leisure activity and as the way to physical fitness. This is reflected in the wide range and diversity of relevant sources of information. Individual enthusiasts have long made their own private collections of all this literature, and now libraries of all types, public, special and academic, have also begun to build up valuable collections. The time is therefore ripe for a systematic guide to information sources and resources in this field, and Richard Cox here gives us the results of his long and assiduous collecting and organising reference to these. The extent of his work is shown by the inclusion of much unexpected material, such as maps and patents, and of resources of great value but less easily accessible, such as the files of local newspapers and theses submitted for Fellowships of the Library Association.

Part II of this major work - the bibliography of secondary works has already been published. This Part I is the Guide to Sources of the bibliographies of secondary and primary sources, and is no mere enumeration: The descriptions are enhanced by perceptive annotations and, where appropriate, equally perceptive criticisms.

Two more parts are promised, and when complete, we shall have a sound foundation for future research and a demonstration of just how many fertile fields await cultivation. Although Dr Cox disclaims an attempt at a systematic structure for his Guide, the arrangement is clear, so that specialists will find no difficulty in arriving at their particular sections, and will owe Richard Cox a considerable debt for providing signposts and gateways to so many interesting fields.

Preface

Although as early as 1801 Joseph Strutt (1) observed that the study of sports and pastimes could provide the means of accurately assessing societies it was not until the 1970s that a significant number of academic historians turned their attentions to sport. Up until then, most sports histories had been written by enthusiasts such as ex-players or officials, journalists or amateur historians for fellow enthusiasts. Although such works differed immensely in accuracy, detail, length and style, typically, they took the form of commentaries on record-breaking performances interspersed with anecdotes evoking the great days of a particular club or a famous sportsman. They were uncritical, concentrated on on-the-field, as opposed to off-the-field activities and, when penned by individuals connected with a particular team or club, 'hyperbolic, chauvinistic, venal or some combination of the above'. (2)

Whilst many early 'academic' histories of sport were essentially social histories, concentrating their attentions on such issues as class conflict and sport as a mechanism of social control, more recent histories employing a wider range of concepts, theories and sources have raised new issues to illuminate our understanding even further. (3)

Although there is much evidence to confirm the view that sports history '... now thrives as a self-conscious discipline attuned to economic causation, to class distinctions and conflicts, to the masses as well as the elites, to cultural continuity as well as change and to sociological and anthropological modes of research and analysis' (4) a barrier to research and scholarship and a motivation for this particular guide is the difficulty experienced by sports historians in identifying and locating suitable source materials. Concern has been expressed at the impact this has had on the direction and quality of research to date. In the introduction to his treatise on the history of sport in Britain, Holt (5) notes the tendency of historians to explore only themes which have been facilitated by the ready availability of sources. Consequently, important areas of research have been totally neglected.

This problem is exacerbated by the fact that no guide to primary sources and record collections, to date, has included discussion/sections on sources for sports history. Numerous guides and bibliographies of sources for railway history, business history, etc. exist but there is nothing specifically concerned with sport. (6) The first edition of the otherwise invaluable guide to *British Archives* compiled by J. Foster and J. Shephard (London: Macmillan, 1982) listed many collections but only three that were concerned primarily with sport. Similarly, the National Register of Archives has recently compiled a list of finding aids in order to assist the researcher ploughing through their more general catalogues when more specialised works already exist in that area. It is interesting to note that no lists are included for, or which embrace sporting sources. (7)

This guide to sources for the history of sport is the first volume of a series of bibliographical aids to meet the growing interest in and demand for information on the history of sport in Britain. It attempts to identify the many different sources primarily for the study of the history of sport in Britain, and to discuss problems associated with their use. Volume Two *Sport in Britain: A Bibliography of Historical Publications* is a comprehensive classified listing of secondary works and was published by Manchester University Press in April 1991. Volume Three, a bibliography of published primary sources is still in preparation, Volume Four, an index to sporting manuscripts in the UK has been completed and is to be published by the British Society of Sport History in association with Sports History Publishing in 1994. Volume Five, a listing of artefacts in special collections is yet to begin.

Although several attempts were made to structure this particular volume, it was finally decided to arrange sources initially by order (i.e. primary or secondary sources) and then by form (i.e. monographs, journal articles, theses, etc.) and then to discuss sources for specific areas of research and topics of investigation. To have centred discussion around approaches to sports history such as cultural, economic, intellectual, social history, etc. or around themes such as sport and class, sport and gender, or around individual sports or groups of activities would have resulted in more overlap and duplication. Since a number of anomolies remain, it is important for the researcher to appreciate that they should not attempt to consult only the sections dealing with sources for their specialist topic of investigation, if indeed it is included as a separate entity, without first reading the discussion of more general source materials in Parts I, II and III. Similarly, users may also benefit from consulting chapters on other specialist topics. A researcher investigating the impact of new technology on the prodution of sporting equipment and the influence this had on the practice of the sport might find useful information contained in monographs, magazines, local directories, trade catalogues, patents and sources for the history of sport and industry, gender and sport, etc.

Originally, I had hoped to include samples of many of the printed sources as does W. B. Stephens *Sources for Local History* (Cambridge University Press, 1981) and which had been the inspiration for this work. Unfortunately, the need to reduce the overall size in order to guarantee publication prevented this. Perhaps in due course I will be in a position to publish these separately in a companion volume.

Since new technologies are coming on stream at an alarming rate, many information services are undergoing radical change, especially in the delivery of their service. Undoubtedly, many new products will be on the market within a short space of time following publication of this work. What information was once only available in hard copy may now be accessible on-line, on CD-ROM, magnetic tape or microfiche. Researchers are advised of this fact.

Finally, I beg the reader's pardon for any important sources of information I have accidentally omitted and any mistakes I have made. Although new information was always coming to light, I had to draw the line somewhere if this work was going to find its way into print at a time when it was most needed. I welcome details of additional useful information and invite suggestions for improvements to any future editions.

Acknowledgements

Many individuals have assisted me in the preparation of this guide. In particular, I would like to thank the many librarians and archivists who have helped inspire me along the way, most unbeknowingly. In the early days, the staff of the Brotherton Library, University of Leeds, were especially helpful. This was continued by staff of the Doe Library, the University of California, Berkeley, the School of Education Library, University of Liverpool, the Beckett Park site library, Leeds Metropolitan University, and more recently, the library staff at Manchester Metropolitan University, UMIST and the University of Manchester. Frequent visits to London were made all the more rewarding as a result of the helpful assistance provided by staff of the British Library (Reference, Offical Publications, Maps and Prints divisions), the Department for Education and the University of London (in particular the staff at the Institute of Historical Research).

On a more personal level, for reading through early drafts of the text and offering constructive advice I am indebted to Chris Harte (Editor, Sports History Publishing), Heather Creaton (Centre for Metropolitan History, University of London Institute of Historical Research), John McIlwaine (Lecturer in Library, Archive and Information Studies, University College, London), Gill Potts, Dr Bill Stephens (formerly Reader in History of Education, University of Leeds), John Tuck (John Rylands University Library Manchester) and Dr Jack Williams (Senior Lecturer in History, John Moore's University, Liverpool). For assistance with preparation of the final manuscript I am grateful to Peter Blore (D'Arc Partnership) and Catherine Croft who patiently tolerated my frequent changes of mind and put me to rights on so many aspects of grammar and style .

Finally, as always, I have my wife to thank for her generous support for yet another time-consuming and expensive project which she was expected to subsidise and tolerate without any personal gain.

Introduction

Subjects chosen for the historical investigation of sport are diverse but generally fall into one or more of three main categories. That is studies of the emergent role of sport and sport related activities within society at large, particular communities or institutions; the development of individual forms of activity or games; and biographical studies of individual teams and personalities. The period over which such topics can be examined also varies enormously. While certain activities have their origins in the ancient civilizations of the Classical World and the Far East, others are only recent inventions.

Sources for the history of sport vary in nature, volume and accessibility depending upon the topic under investigation. What is important for the historian of sport is to identify the most appropriate sources for the subject of his research. The most appropriate sources are generally those which are accessible, reliable and most revealing of significant, pertinent information. The sources appropriate for the investigation of different topics vary immensely and may also differ for the study of the same subject at different stages/period of their development/ evolution. While an investigation of the BBC's television presentation of the Olympic Games will rely heavily on systematic examination of hours of recorded video tape, a study of the contribution of Thomas Arnold to the emergence of athleticism in the Victorian public school will rely upon careful examination of his writings in the form of diaries, sermons, etc. and the contemporary views expressed by those around him. Similarly, a study of the emergence of sports medicine may demand extracting evidence from amphora, papyri and inscriptions during the Classical period and monographs, periodical articles and unpublished patient medical records for the modern era. Generally speaking, sources for the history of sport in Britain became increasingly more common with the passing of time. We also move from a period in which we have records alluding to sport to a period in which we have records of sporting bodies themselves. Researchers of Roman Britain may be as dependent upon the work of the archaelogist's spade and trowel as upon the written word of contemporaries, and it is not until the modern period that the sports historian witnesses references to sport other than purely by chance. This is not to suggest that information does not exist: Anglo-Saxon chronicles, the Bayeux Tapestry, Borough Charters, Coroner's Rolls, the rolls of itinerant justices, the Close Rolls, the Patent Rolls, the Liberate Rolls, Rolls of Monasterial Courts, Manorial Court Rolls, Borough Court of Assembly. Books have been found to contain pertinent information for the historian of Medieval Sport. The simple fact is that the researchers of earlier periods are obliged to piece together scraps of information from an array of fragmented evidence in order to complete the picture.

Social historians of sport have illustrated the importance of studying wider issues taking place in society at large. In an article entitled "Physiologists, Physicians and Physical Educators: Nineteenth Century Biology and Exercise, Hygiene and Education', R. J. Park (8) draws attention to the significance of contemporary scientific thought in interpreting changing attitudes towards physical training and care of the body. Similarly, K. A. P. Sandiford in a paper on "Cricket and the Victorians' (9) draws attention to changes in horticultural practice and technology to explain some of the changes that took place in the organisation and practice of cricket in the late nineteenth century. Others have illustrated the importance of the prevailing religious beliefs, (10) political ideologies (11) and the economy. (12) In other words, the social historian of sport, as opposed to the 'antiquarian' or 'chronologer', (13) will be in search of information not only about sport, but on related (directly and indirectly) socio-political-economic circumstances. Information requirements will also vary according to the perspective applied to the topic under investigation. Historians have often found it helpful to draw upon perspectives, methods, concepts and models borrowed from other academic disciplines such as anthropology, (14) archaeology, (15) economics, (16) philosophy, (17) psychology, (18) geography, (19) literature (20) and sociology, (21) in which case they may require information on the perspectives and methods of the discipline itself. Contemporary evidence sought will also have a different emphasis. An economic historian of sport, for example, is likely to be more interested in financial records to identify significant changes and explain their causes, whilst an art historian will be more interested in the changing images of sport as reflected through contemporary paintings and other works of fine art.

Because of the diverse range of source material available to the sports historian, it is difficult to make many generalisations and therefore to discuss them as an homogenous whole. Nevertheless, it is probably true to claim that all such sources can be divided into either primary or secondary forms and it is under these headings that sports history information will now be discussed. Primary sources may be thought of as original forms of documentation, presenting facts as they were witnessed first-hand, whilst secondary sources are generally regarded as those expressing the views and interpretations of commentators on past events and personalities. Primary sources can include written documents in the form of coaching manuals, diaries, score books, committee minutes, accounts, etc; pictorial records in the form of prints, photographs, films, drawings, paintings and sketches; oral recordings in the form of disks and magnetic tape; items of clothing and equipment etc. Secondary sources include treatises in the form of books, journal articles, conference papers, theses, etc. There are obviously a few grey areas, a typical example being a newspaper report. Whilst a recording of a past event, it may be that it was written by a commentator who consciously or unconsciously had a vested interest or a biased attitude of mind that caused him to be selective in what he reported upon and the way in which they interpreted what was actually happening. The sports journalist reporting on his favourite team's performance in a major competition may fail to notice the weaknesses in his side or refuse to accept what many others would consider to be underhand/unsporting tactics. Indeed, he may not consider it to be important to report any negative aspects of play or off-the-ball incidents. A trained historian will automatically know to check the authenticity and reliability of a given source before accepting it as valid evidence. This is achieved by comparing it with other sources and taking into account the background and possible motivations of the commentator.

Since to discuss the sources for all sports in all nations throughout history would be an impossible undertaking, the emphasis (but not exclusive focus) of this guide will be on material in the English language, on sport in the UK, especially during the modern period of history. This is the area in which the author is particularly experienced. Reference is made to guides, collections, sources and histories of sport in the ancient world and overseas for a number of reasons. First of all, a wider objective of this guide is to help promote research in sports history worldwide, regardless of sport, nation or period of investigation. Sports historians researching the development of sport in other countries should get a feel for the range of sources available for their use and may be able to adopt similar strategies to information gathering using sister/parallel publications. Secondly, sports history has attracted greater attention in some overseas countries than it has in Britain with the result that some of the best and indeed only examples of histories, indexes, etc. are to be drawn from those countries. Thirdly, certain developments in sport in the ancient world or in the modern period overseas (e.g. 'the Packer affair') have had a major impact on sport in Britain and it is sometimes important for the sport historian to research these developments where they took place in order to better understand changes on the home front. Finally, several sports historians have expressed an interest in the export of sporting traditions from Britain to the rest of the world and they will require a working knowledge of developments and sources for the history of sport overseas.

It is appreciated that gaps appear within this guide, for example detailed discussion of sources for the history of sport in the ancient world and in Medieval society. This is because valuable works already exist, (as is the case for sport in the Ancient World, see p. 31) or because the author is unfamiliar with useful sources that might exist. Hopefully, any such gaps will soon come to light so that they can be included in future editions of the guide.

Before starting the search for information, it is important to establish exactly what type and range of material is required. It may be that only basic factual information is required; a rule, name, date of birth, score, average or result. This kind of information can often be found in quick reference works such as encyclopaedias, biographical dictionaries, chronologies or statistical compilations. An individual requiring further detail, perhaps with a discussion of the factors bringing about certain changes, will find it necessary to extend his search to monographs, journal articles and possibly theses. Researchers working at the forefront of their field may also require details of recently published and ongoing research. To identify this kind of information the researcher will be required to search various on-line bibliographic databases, indexes to conference proceedings, directories of current research and catalogues of forthcoming publications.

To appreciate the relationship between different bibliographical aids, some of the problems associated with their use and strategies for effectively interrogating them, the reader is advised to consult the author's article on "A Model for Sports History Documentation' in the *International Journal of the History of Sport*, 9, 2 (August, 1992), 252-279.

General Guides To Sources of Information

General guides to sources of information which will help the researcher identify other reference works, including indexes to different forms of publication, include: P.W. Lea *Printed Reference Material* (3rd edition) (London: Library Association, 1990); E. P. Sheehy *Guide to Reference Books* (10th edition) (Chicago: American Library Association, 1986); R. E. Stevens and L. C. Smith *Reference Works in the University Library* (Littleton, CO: Libraries Unlimited, 1986); A. J. Walford *Guide to Reference Material* (4th edition) (London: The Library Association, 1982-86) (22) (vols 2 Social and Historical Sciences and 3 - Generalia); S. Kirkham *How To Find Information in the Humanities* (London: Bingley, 1989) and G. Chandler *How To Find Out* (5th edition) (Oxford: Pergamon, 1982). Sheehy and Stevens have a North American bias and although limited in which reference works they include about sport, are useful for identifying literature in other fields such as biography, Government publications, etc. These works may be updated, to some extent, by *American Reference Books Annual* (Littleton, CO: Libraries Unlimited) and *Reference Books Bulletin* (American Library Association) which announce new publications.

Guides specific to one particular subject area of potential value to the sports historian include: A. E. Day *History: A Reference Handbook* (London: Bingley, 1977), P. Hepworth *How To Find Out In History: A Guide To Sources of Information For All* (Oxford: Pergamon, 1966); Helen Poulton *Historian's Handbook: A Descriptive Guide to Reference Works* (Norman, OK: University of Oklahoma Press, 1972); T. F. Tingley *Social History of the United States: A Guide To Information Sources* (Detroit, MI: Gale Research Co., 1979); B. Gratch, B. Chan and J. Lingenfelter *Sport and Physical Education: A Guide to Reference Resources* (Westport, CT: Greenwood Press, 1983), R. J. Higgs *Sport: A Guide to Reference Sources* (Westport, CT: Greenwood Press, 1983) and Ray Prytherch *Sports and Fitness: An Information Guide* (Aldershot: Gower, 1988). Unfortunately, all of the history guides are now considerably out-of-date and in need of updating. In terms of sports literature, Gratch et al and Higgs are more comprehensive than Prytherch but have a North American bias. Whereas Gratch et al's work is a straightforward listing of reference works (with some brief annotations) associated with individual sports followed by subject discipline areas, Higgs' guide includes bibliographical essays on popular sporting themes. Both have their place in the sports historian's library, although Gratch et al's work should reach a wider audience since it includes details of publications not written specifically for an academic readership.

Guides to sources of information on specific sporting activities include: A. Grobani *Guide To [American] Football Literature* (Detroit, MI: Gale Research Co., 1975) and *Guide To Baseball Literature* (Detroit, MI: Gale Research Co., 1976); A. Lumpkin *Guide To The Literature of Tennis* (Westport, CT: Greenwood Press, 1985); D. A. Peel *Racket and Paddle Games: A Guide to Information Sources* (Detroit, MI: Gale Research Co., 1980) and B. Wischria and M. Post *Running: A Guide To The Literature* (New York: Garland, 1980). Unfortunately, none of these publications are very broad in scope. They are biased towards North American material. The only British guides of a similar nature are D. R. Allen *A Catalogue of Cricket Catalogues, Booklists, Bibliographical Sources and Indexes Etcetera* (reprinted from the *Journal of the Cricket Society*, vols 8-9, (1978-79) and D. Kennington *Sourcebook of Golf* (London: Library Association, 1980) the latter of which provides only a smattering of the source material available to the researcher. Occasionally, brief guides to sports literature are included in periodical articles prepared primarily to assist librarians in their work. An example is J. I. Ozmert "The History of Horse Racing and its Literature', *AB Bookman's Weekly*, 80 (July, 1987), 5-12.

Part I - Quick Reference Material
Encyclopaedias and Dictionaries

For the historian requiring only basic factual information about a particular sport, event, club or personality, a dictionary or encyclopaedia might supply all the information that is required. General encyclopaedias, such as the *Encyclopaedia Britannica*, contain significant sections on most sports including details of important events, personalities and results that have been influential or provided significant turning points in their history. An abstract of a paper entitled *"The Encyclopaedia Britannica in Teaching and Researching Sports History'* by R.C. Thurmond published in the *NASSH Proceedings* of 1973 (pp. 40-41) illustrates some of the merits of this particular publication.

There are many dictionaries of history, some focusing on specific periods, others on particular nations, some a mixture of the two. Generally speaking, the more specialised the title of the dictionary the more detail contained on related topics within, although the volume and amount of detail will usually vary from subject to subject, often according to the knowledge and enthusiasm of the compiler. Cuddon (see below), for example, includes twenty five pages on cricket but far fewer on most other sports.

Examples of a few of the many historical dictionaries which may prove useful to the sports historian include: A. W. Palmer *Dictionary of Modern History, 1789-1945* (Harmondsworth: Penguin, 1977) and F. E. Huggett *A Dictionary of British History, 1815-1973* (Oxford: Blackwells, 1974).

Useful sports dictionaries (23) and encyclopaedias include: John Arlott *Oxford Companion to Sports and Games* (London: Oxford University Press, 1975); F. G. Menke *The Encylopaedia of Sports* (6th edition) (Brunswick, NJ: A. S. Barnes, 1977); D. Matz *Greek and Roman Sport: A Dictionary of Athletes and Events from the Eighth Century BC to the Third Century AD* (Jefferson, NC: McFarland and Co., 1991), R. Hickok *New Encyclopaedia of Sports* (New York: McGraw-Hill, 1977) and W.Vamplew *The Oxford Companion to Australian Sport* (Melbourne: Oxford University Press, 1992). These sources may be considered the best sports encyclopaedias for background historical information. Typically, the article for each sport begins with a history followed by famous players and outstanding records. D. P. Blaine *An Encyclopaedia of Rural Sports* (London: Longmans, 1840) and H. C. Howard (Earl of Suffolk), H. Peak and F. G. Aflalo *The Encyclopaedia of Sport* (London: Lawrence and Bullen, 1911) (both of which ran to more than one edition) are amongst the most useful for the historian researching early developments of sport in Britain. There are also a large number of sport specific encyclopaedias. Publishers Robert Hale produced a useful series in the 1960s and 70s which included volumes on: association football, athletics, boxing, cricket, flat racing, motor racing, rugby football, rugby league football, show jumping and swimming, some of which ran to several editions. More recently, Guinness Superlatives have produced encyclopaedic works which are updated regularly, although under different series titles . The recent Facts Series includes, so far, volumes on cricket, golf, motorcycling, mountains and mountaineering, rugby, soccer and yachting. In terms of sports dictionaries, J. A. Cuddon *Macmillan Dictionary of Sports and Games* (London: Macmillan, 1980) is probably the most useful to the sports historian. M. Rundell *The Dictionary of Cricket* (London: Bloomsbury, 1985) is an informative mixture of history, etymology and social comment.

Other, more specialist reference works are: R. Bateman *Encyclopaedia of Sports Stamps* (London: Stanley Paul, 1969), B. Liddle *Dictionary of Sporting Quotations* (London: R.K.P., 1987) and M. Brander (London: A. and C. Black, 1968). All these and other such publications relating to sport in Britain published before 31/12/1988 are listed in R. W. Cox *Sport in Britain,* (updated in the *Bulletin of the Society of the History of Sport.* 1988-92; *The Sports Historian,* 1993 onwards). A review of select, mainly North American sports encyclopaedias by D. A. Peele is included in *Reference Services Review,* 10 (Fall, 1982), 61-63.

Almanacs, Chronologies, Statistical Compilations, Directories, Handbooks and Yearbooks

Some governing bodies of sport and publishers produce yearbooks, directories or almanacs which usually contain hoards of factual information. Probably, the most famous of these is *Wisden Cricketers'*

Almanack published annually (currently by John Wisden and Co.) since 1864. This publication includes details of cricketing records, including the results of all the previous year's major competitions; fixtures for the forthcoming season; up-to-date information on rules, new publications on cricket, deaths of cricketers, etc. *An Index to Wisden Cricketers' Almanack, 1864-1984* (London: Queen Anne Press) was complied by D. Barnard. This can be particularly helpful in scanning a hundred and twenty years' worth of *Wisden* for information on specific individuals. In 1970, Rothmans started their *Football Yearbook*, one year later their *Rugby Union Yearbook* and in 1980, the *Rothmans' Rugby League Yearbook*. In the mid 1980s, Newnes started a new series of yearbooks published in association with certain governing bodies of sport such as the Football Association and the British Board of Boxing Control. Other useful serials of a similar nature include: *Baily's Hunting Directory* (published annually since 1897), *The Golfer's Handbook* (published annually since 1903) and the *British Rowing Almanac* (published annually since 1860). Many more directories containing varying amounts of detail exist for association football, cricket and rugby. CBD Research of Beckenham publish periodically a guide to *Current British Directories*, which may help the researcher track down additional sources of interest. In 1992, CBD also published a *Directory of European Sports Organisations*.

Finally, a number of directories of sports grounds have been published in recent years which include potted histories of each of the venues included. Examples include T. Delaney *The Grounds of Rugby League* (Keighley: Delaney, 1991), G. Plumtree *Homes of Cricket: The First Class Grounds of England and Wales* (London: Macdonald, 1988), S. P. Inglis *The Football Grounds of Great Britain* (London: Collins Willow, 1988) W. A. Powell *The Wisden Guide to Cricket Grounds* (London: Stanley Paul, 1992) and A. Sampson *Winning Waters* (London: Hale, 1986).

Sometimes the researcher will require specific factual information about the date of a given event, the cost of living at a particular time, details of attendance figures at certain fixtures, etc. In addition to the encyclopaedias, directories and yearbooks mentioned above, several other publications may be useful in this respect.

Many historical chronologies have been published containing varying amounts of detail. The Penguin series provides a relatively inexpensive, handy guide to dates. Volumes exist for the *Ancient World* by H. E. L. Mellersh, *The Medieval World, 800-1491* by R. L. Storey, *The Expanding World, 1492-1762* by N. Williams and *The Modern World, 1763-1965* also by N. Williams. An up-to-the-minute diary of world events is *Keesing's Record of Contemporary Events* (formerly Keesing's Contemporary Archive) (London: Longman) published weekly from 1931 until 1983 and monthly since then. This publication lists important events in all countries, including texts of speeches, obituaries, statistics, etc. and has a very full set of cumulative indexes. For a review of current issues in Britain, *Contemporary Britain: An Annual Review,* edited by P. Catterall and published for the Institute of Contemporary British History by Blackwell Publishers annually since 1990, is a fine publication. It provides both a detailed record of the year, and an in-depth scrutiny of events and issues, their context and the policy responses, adopted. Each of the three volumes published to date critically assesses current concerns and the prevailing trends and themes in British sport during the year. These have been written by sports historian, P. Bilsborough.

The only major chronology of sports history identified by the author as applicable to the history of sport in Britain is the *Daten zur Sportgeschichte* series compiled by K. C. Wilt published in Stuttgart by Verlag Karl Hofman in the 1970s (vol. 1 *Die Alte Welt und Europa bis 1750*, vol. 2 *Europa von 1750 bis 1894*, vol. 3 *Nord und Latinamerika bis 1900*). Perhaps it is worth pointing out that a number of sports history books include chronologies of significant dates and events in appendices. J. Berryman compiled a lengthy chronology in R. J. Higgs *Sport: A Reference Handbook* (Westport, CT: Greenwood Press, 1983), J. Ford a chronology of boxing in *Prize Fighting: The Age of Regency Boximania* (Newton Abbot: David and Charles, 1971), R. Bowen includes a chronology of cricket in *Cricket: A History of Its Growth and Development Throughout the World* (London: Eyre and Spottiswoode, 1970); U. A. Titley and N. McWhirter a chronology of rugby union in their *Centenary History of the Rugby Football Union* (London: Rugby Football Union, 1970).

What was intended to be an annual review of the year's major sporting events started in 1979 under the title *Sports Facts: Results, Records and Figures*. Compiled by G. Edge and K. Walmsley, this useful listing of major events, stories, records and results appears to have lasted only a couple of years.

Background information and statistics on such topics as education, population, and trade, in individual countries, worldwide, can be gleaned from the *Statesman's Yearbook* (London: Macmillan) published annually since 1863.

Useful compilations of historical statistics include: B. R. Mitchell *British Historical Statistics* (Cambridge: Cambridge University Press, 1988)*European Historical Statistics, 1750-1975* (2nd edition) (London: Macmillan, 1980), and A. H. Halsey *British Social Trends Since 1900* (London, Macmillan, 1984). The first of these is probably the principal reference guide with statistics ranging from the twelfth century to the start of the 1980s. The second listed volume is useful because of the comparative material it contains. More recent data is provided in the Macmillan *British Historical Facts Series* and *Abstracts of British Historical Statistics* series. Vamplew in his economic history of sport in Britain *Pay Up and Play the Game* (Cambridge: Cambridge University Press, 1989) uses price indices from *Abstracts of British Historical Statistics* in order to allow the reader to convert prices, costs, turnover, earnings and investment figures into modern equivalents. Although none of these publications deal specifically with sport, they do contain background information on such topics as wages, standard of living, population, etc. which may be useful to the social historian of sport. Non-specialist series of statistics which do document sporting statistics (although only for recent times and to differing extents) include: *Sponsorship Report* (Mintell), *Social Trends* (CSO), *Spending on Sport and Leisure by Local Government* (CIPFA) and the *UK Household Survey* (OPCS).

Statistical publications devoted specifically to sport include: *The Hamlyn A - Z Series of Records* (which includes volumes on Cricket and Soccer), *The Guinness Book of Olympic Records, The Guinness Book of British and Empire and Commonwealth Games Records* and *The Guinness Book of Sports Records, Winners and Champions*. For recent statistics of sport, including details of participation rates, numbers of clubs affiliated to the Governing Bodies, sales figures for equipment, etc., the Sports Council (London: The Sports Council, 1993) may be of some use. For individual sports there are several useful publications (in addition to the encyclopaedias and Guinness *Facts and Feats Series* mentioned above) especially relating to association football, athletics, cricket, golf and rugby. Those published before the end of 1988 are listed in R. W. Cox (1991). Especially useful for details of attendance figures, scores, league tables, averages and other such information are the publications of The Association of Football Statisticians & Historians, The Association of Cricket Statisticians & Historians and The Association of Track and Field Statisticians. The Football Trust publish a *Digest of Football Statistics* periodically.

Finally, the government, primarily through the Central Office of Information, publishes a large amount of statistical data on a whole range of topics, some of which might provide useful background information for the sports historian. Details of official statistics are provided in the Central Statistical Office *Guide to Official Statistics* (5th edition) (London: HMSO, 1986), of unofficial statistics in D. Mort and L. Siddall *Unofficial Statistics* (Aldershot: Gower, 1985). The latter provides a useful guide to the statistics produced by a whole range of bodies such as nationalised industries, professional institutions, banks, academic bodies, trade unions, Chambers of Commerce and so on.

Subject Bibliographies (Including Bibliographical Essays and Bibliographical Series)

The literature associated with certain sports and events is reasonably well documented in the form of bibliographies. Unfortunately, published bibliographies are always out-of-date by the time they appear in print and will need to be updated using some of the reference works listed in this chapter. Certain bibliographies are regularly updated and some may be accessed on-line. All bibliographies are restricted to specific forms of publications (monographs, periodical articles, conference proceedings, theses, etc.); periods in history (Medieval, Victorian, etc.); activity(ies) (ball games, water sports, cricket, etc.); geographical region (North America, Yorkshire, etc.); religion, race or gender; country, period of publication; standard of scholarship (academic, popular, etc.); language of publication; library collection or some combination of the above. (24) Hence, it is often necessary to extend one's search beyond existing bibliographies in which case it is important to plan a search strategy that will cover the 'missing gaps' (not already covered by indexes and other reference works) and also avoid as much duplication as possible. (25)

Many bibliographies, although very few specifically relating to sport, can be identified using T. Besterman *World Bibliography of Bibliographies* (five vols) (Lausanne: Societas Bibliographica, 1966) followed by A. F. Toomey *World Bibliography of Bibliographies, 1964-1974* (two vols) (Totowa, NJ: Rowman and Littlefield, 1977). These two publications can be updated using *Bibliographic Index*, a cumulative bibliography of bibliographies containing more than fifty citations published separately as well as in books, pamphlets and journal articles. This index is arranged by subject and is published quarterly and in yearly volumes by H. W. Wilson since 1938.

For the thirty years prior to his death in 1991, sports historian Emeritus Professor Seward Staley at the University of Illinois, Champaign, had been compiling a bibliography of sports bibliographies. Although no published works have so far emerged from the project there are presently several thousand bibliographies which have been identified, described and listed. At the time of writing, this information is in the custody of the University of Illinois Press.

Several bibliographies and bibliographical series on history have been produced. By far the most comprehensive is *Historical Abstracts* (Oxford: ABC-Clio), published three times a year since 1955, with annual and five yearly cumulative author and subject indexes. *Historical Abstracts* includes abstracts of periodical articles, selected conference proceedings, books and dissertations on the modern history of all parts of the world. These are published in two parts. Part A: *Modern Abstracts, 1450-1914* and Part B: *Twentieth Century Abstracts*. *Historical Abstracts* can be searched on-line back to 1973 through DIALOG. Generated from entries in this database is: *Bibliographies in History: An Index to Bibliographies in Journals and Dissertations Covering All Countries of the World Except the US and Canada* (Oxford: Clio, 1988). Compiled for the Bibliography Committee of the International Committee of Historical Sciences and sponsored by UNESCO *The International Bibliography of Historical Sciences* has been published (currently by Saur) annually (with the exception of 1940-46) since 1926. It provides a survey of the more important histories published in a given year. Unfortunately, it is highly selective, difficult to use (in that it does not include a subject index) and usually several years out of date by the time it appears in print. Very few items on sports history have so far been included. During the 1960s and early 70s Cambridge University Press published the *Conference on British Studies Bibliographical Handbooks Series* which includes volumes on: *Anglo Norman England, 1066-1154* by M. Altschul (1969); *Tudor England, 1485-1603* by M. Levine (1968); *The Seventeenth Century* by D. Berkowitz (1970); *Restoration England, 1660-1689* by W. L. Sachse (1971); *Victorian England, 1837-1901* by J. L. Altholz (1970) and *Twentieth Century England* by A. Havinghurst (1970). Again very few items on sport are included.

The Royal Historical Society in conjunction with the American Historical Association, published an extensive series of Bibliographies of British History (Oxford: Clarendon Press) which list books and articles, with annotations, published up to the time when the bibliographies themselves were completed. Volumes include: *Tudor Period, 1485-1603* by C. Read (1959); *Stuart Period, 1603-1714* (2nd edition) by M. F. Keeler (1970); *The Eighteenth Century, 1714-1789* by S. Pargellis and D. J. Medley (1951); *1789-1815* by L. M. Brown and I. Christie (1977), *1815-1914* by H. J. Hanham (1976). Unlike the *British Studies Bibliographical Handbook Series*, a large number of references on sports and pastimes are included. Recently, a new project was sponsored by the Royal Historical Society to document literature on the history of Britain. The project is based at the University of Cambridge and it is hoped to complete the task in 1994.

The Royal Historical Society and the Institute of Historical Research have also produced a valuable bibliographical series entitled *Writings on British History*. These volumes provide a bibliography of books and articles on the history of Great Britain from 450 AD to 1939, published anywhere in the world in any language (except Russian and Japanese) during the years covered (ie. 1901-1933, 1934, etc.). A small number of publications on the history of sport are included although these are not listed as a separate category, but under the miscellany section of publications on Economic and Social History. Volumes published cover the years 1901-1933 (Auxiliary Sciences and General Works (1968), The Middle Ages, 450-1485) (1968), The Tudor and Stuart Periods, 1485-1714 (1968), The Eighteenth Century, 1714-1815 (1969), 1815-1914 (1970); vol. 2 1934 (1937); vol. 3 1935 (1939); vol. 4 1936 (1940); vol. 5 1937 (1949); vol. 6 1938 (1951); vol. 7 1939 (1953); vol. 8 1940-45 (1960); vol. 9 1946-48 (1973); vol. 10 1949-51 (1975); vol. 11 1952-54 (1975); vol. 12 1955-57 (1977); vol. 13 1958-59 (1977); vol. 14 1960-61 (1978); vol. 15 1962-64 (1979); vol. 16 1965-66 (1981); vol. 17 1967-68 (1982); vol. 18 1969-70 (1984); vol. 19 1971-72 (1985); vol. 20 1973-74 (1986). This publication is succeeded by the Royal Historical Society *Annual Bibliography of British and Irish History* which has been published since 1976 (for the year 1975) (Hassocks: Harvester). Some items on sport have found their way into the publication under the heading Intellectual and Cultural History, but these reflect only a very select few. Although the bibliography aims at comprehensive coverage, unfortunately, no criteria are disclosed for what is and what is not included, preventing the researcher from knowing how much further to cast his net in search of appropriate material.

The Institute of Contemporary British History recently sponsored an annotated bibliography of *British History, 1945-87*, which was published by Blackwells in 1991. Included in this highly comprehensive work are sections on sport in England, Scotland, Ireland and Wales.

The University of London's Institute of Historical Research once published five yearly *Bibliographies of Historical Works Issued in the United Kingdom*. The first volume covered the years 1940-45 and was published in 1947, the last volume to be published covered the years 1970-75. This bibliographical series listed works on the history of any subject or nation published in Britain within the years covered by the different volumes. The Historical Association *Annual Bibliography of Historical Literature* (1911 onwards) critically reviews a selection of the previous year's major publications with different reviewers for each of the different periods and subjects covered. Unfortunately, to date, very few histories of sport have been included although this might change in future years as sports history becomes more popular and accepted as a legitimate branch of social history. Single bibliographies listing useful background reading on social history but very little specifically on sport are: W. H. Chaloner and R. C. Richardson *British Economic and Social History: A Bibliographic Guide* (2nd edition) (Manchester: Manchester University Press, 1984) and J. Roach *Bibliography of British Social History* (Cambridge: Cambridge University Press, 1974).

Ongoing bibliographies directly concerned with the history of sport are: "The Annual Bibliography of Publications on the History of Sport' (published annually in the December edition of the *International Journal of History of Sport* (1984 onwards) (which lists scholarly works) and various bibliographies and lists ("Book News', "Journal Surveys', "Recent Dissertations') published occasionally in the *Journal of Sport History* since the first issue in 1984. Other historical bibliographical series, containing useful background reading material and occasional references on sports history are divided into three main types and include:

(a) Period bibliographies, e.g. *International Medieval Bibliography* (Published three times a year since 1967 by the Department of History at the University of Leeds); *Sixteenth Century Bibliography* (St Louis, MO: St Louis Centre for Reformation Research); *The Eighteenth Century: A Current Bibliography* (published annually by AMS Press, New York since 1974); "Victorian Bibliography' (published annually in *Victorian Studies* since 1957).

(b) Discipline/Method bibliographies, e.g. "List of Publications on the Economic and Social History of Great Britain and Ireland', published annually since 1927 in *Economic History Review*; "Current British Work' in *Oral History* (published since 1972); "Current Bibliography of Urban History' (published annually in the *Urban History Yearbook* since 1974); and "The Bibliography of British Labour History' (published annually in the *Bulletin of the Society for the Study of Labour History* since

1960); "Recent Publications in Local History' (published annually since 1952 in *Local Historian*) and

(c) Area bibliographies, based on individual countries - e.g. "Articles Relating to the History of Wales' (published annually in *Welsh Historical Review* since 1960); regions - e.g. "Review of Periodical Literature and Occasional Publications' (published annually in *Northern History* since 1964); or cities, e.g. "London Bibliography' (published annually in *The London Journal* since 1975).

Other historical bibliographical series containing useful background reading can be identified in D. Henige *Serial Bibliographies and Abstracts in History: An Annotated Guide* (Bibliographies and Indexes in World History Series No. 2) (Westport, CT: Greenwood Press, 1986).

Bibliographical series devoted exclusively to sport and occasionally including items of a historical nature are:

Sports Bibliography (Ottawa, Sports Information Resource Centre, 1982) an eight volume index to literature on all aspects of sport. This includes scholarly works in the form of monographs, periodical articles, conference papers and theses accepted for higher degrees (mainly in North America). Volume 7 covers the Humanities and Social Sciences and devotes thirty pages of references to 'Halls of Fame', 'Historical Research' and 'Historiography', and 'History' (in individual countries). In addition to providing author and title indexes this bibliography indicates the academic level of each entry. Documents are assigned a basic, intermediate or advanced level code which may benefit the professional historian only interested in reading analytical, referenced works. Updates have been produced in subsequent years and the bibliography is now available on CD-ROM as *Sports Discus* (distributed by Silver Platter Information Ltd). It may be accessed on-line via DIALOG. Both the hard-back and CD-ROM versions are updated by *Sports Search* a monthly index produced by the Sports Information Resource Centre.

Until recently, SIRLS, the sociology of leisure and sport database based at the University of Waterloo, published *Sport and Leisure: A Journal of Social Science Abstracts* (formerly *Sociology and Leisure Abstracts* 1980-1988) and maintained an on-line data base accessible remotely via Datapac, the Canadian Telecommunications system. Up until 1979, they also maintained standard files which were regularly updated, two of which were devoted to sports history (File 38 - *Sociology of Sport and Leisure - Renaissance to Modern Times* and File 39 - *Sociology of Sport and Leisure - Ancient and Medieval Times*). These files provide useful bibliographies and are still available in a number of libraries (e.g. John Rylands University Library Manchester). They may be updated using *Sociology of Leisure Abstracts* (1980-87) and *Sport and Leisure* (1988-1990). At the time of writing, this database is in the process of being transferred to the Sports Information Resource Centre at Ottawa where it will be integrated into *Sports Discus* and available from the Autumn of 1993.

Completed Research in Health, Physical Education, Recreation and Dance (published annually in Reston, VA by the American Alliance for Health, Physical Education, Recreation and Dance since 1953) provides an index to theses and dissertations completed in a number of North American universities and periodical articles appearing in a select list of professional physical education journals.

'One-off' bibliographies of note, devoted to specific sports include: F. Lake and H. Wright *Bibliography of Archery* (Manchester: Simon Simon Archery Foundation, 1974), E. W. Padwick *Bibliography of Cricket* (2nd edition) (London: The Library Association in association with J. W. McKenzie (Bookseller) on behalf of the Cricket Society, 1984) and its supplement compiled by S. Ely and P. Griffiths, (26) J. S. Murdock *Library of Golf 1743-1966* (Detroit, MI: Gale Research Co., 1968), D. McLaren *A Handbook of Rugby Literature* (2nd edition) (1990) T. McNab and P. Lovesey *Guide To British Track and Field Literature 1275-1968* (London: Athletics Arena, 1969). More general bibliographies, including references on sport history are: E. B. Wells *Horsemanship: A Bibliography of Printed Material From the 16th Century* (New York: Garland, 1985) and A. Grimshaw *The Horse: A Bibliography of British Books 1851-1976* (London: The Library Association, 1982).

Bibliographical essays and literature reviews on sports history which tend to review and evaluate rather than simply list or annotate or abstract important works on a given subject are: W. J. Baker "The Leisure Revolution of Victorian England: A Review of Recent Literature', *Journal of Sport History*, 6, 3 (Winter, 1979), 76-86; J. M. Carter "All Work and No Play? A Review of the Literature of Medieval Sport', *Canadian Journal of the History of Sport and Physical Education*, 11, 2 (December, 1980), 67-72 and R. D. Mandell "The Modern Olympic Games: A Bibliographical Essay', *Sportwissenschaft*, 6, 1 (1976), 89-97.

These and other bibliographies of value to the sports historian studying developments in Britain and published before 31/12/1988 are listed in R. W. Cox (1991) and updated in *The British Society of Sports Bulletin* (1988-1992) and *The Sports Historian* (1993-).

Scholarly histories of sport, including unpublished theses, often contain bibliographical reviews or detailed bibliographies which can be useful to the researcher. Good examples include W. J. Baker "Sources and Suggested Readings' in his *Sports in the Western World* (Totowa, NJ: Rowman and Littlefield, 1983) pp. 341-355 and A. Guttmann "Bibliographical Essay' in his *A Whole New Ball Game: An Interpretation of American Sports* (Chapel Hill, NC: The University of North Carolina Press, 1988), pp. 209-219. The researcher should always be aware that such bibliographies may sometimes be highly selective intentionally or otherwise and would be advised to extend their research to additional sources in most instances.

Finally, a number of useful bibliographies on sport have been compiled for Fellowships of the Library Association (FLA). Titles highlighting sport include: B. C. Skilling *British Canoeing Literature, January 1866 - January, 1966: A Bibliography and Subject Guide* (1967); E. P. Loder *Bibliography of the History and Organisation of Horse Racing and Thoroughbred Breeding in Great Britain and Ireland* (1975); B. J. Read *Mountaineering, The Literature in English: A Classified Bibliography* (1976).

Many regional bibliographies (see p. 55) accepted for FLA also include references on sport. FLA theses may be identified using P. J. Taylor *FLA Theses: Abstracts of all Theses Accepted for Fellowship of the Library Association from 1964* (London: British Library, 1979) and for more recent works the catalogue of the Library Association Library. Again, those related to sport in Britain published before 31/12/1988 are listed in R. W. Cox (1991) and updated in the *British Society of Sports History Bulletin* (1988-92) and *The Sports Historian* (1993-).

An important point to appreciate in using some bibliographies and bibliographical series, especially those commercially produced, is that the contents of one bibliography is simply a sub-set of another. Clio Press for example, generates numerous bibliographies compiled from the same database. Thus it would be futile to scan C. E. Harrison *Women in American History: A Bibliography* (Santa Barbara, CA: Clio Press, 1980) if *America: History and Life* had already been searched, in hardback or on-line. This bibliography along with many others in the Clio Bibliographical Series, have simply been downloaded from *America: History and Life* database. The same is true of several other bibliographies (see R. W. Cox's review of L. G. Davis *Joe Louis: A Bibliography* in the *International Journal of the History of Sport*, 5, 1 (May, 1988), pp.589-81.

Citation Indexes

Citation indexes are a rather different kind of indexing service. They work on the principal that, if there is one reference known to be relevant for the search in hand, it can be looked up and the citation index volume will list details of other publications citing it. These in turn can be looked up in the source index volume, leading to more references. Publications on specific topics can be traced through the permutation subject index volume. The only citation index that might be of any real value to the sports historian is *Arts and Humanities Index* (Philadelphia, PA: Institute for Scientific Information, 1976 to date). Published three times a year, this data base is also available online as *Arts and Humanities Search*. (Also see p. 20.)

Other Reference Works

Further reference sources of potential interest to the sports historian include: D. Booker *Directory of Scholars Identifying With the History of Sport* (4th edition) (College Park, PA: North American Society of Sports Historians, 1988) and P. Ray *Rothmans' Atlas of World Sports* (Aylesbury: Rothmans, 1982). The directory provides details of the names, addresses, research interests, recent publications and professional affiliations of sports historians. Although coverage is international, there is a strong North American bias.

A highly selective review list of recently published reference works is contained in C. G. Hoover "Sports Reference Books', *Booklist*, 85 (March, 1989), 1260-3.

Part II - Secondary Sources

Monographs

Secondary sources in the form of monographs and anthologies may be be identified or located by first identifying pertinent library collections using directories such as B. T. Darnay *Directory of Special Libraries and Information Centres* (11th edition) (Detroit, MI: Gale Research, 1988) (A reference guide, published in three volumes, to major collections throughout North America with subject and geographical indexes), R. Lewanski *Subject Collections in European Libraries* (2nd edition) (London: Bowker, 1978); the *Aslib Guide to Sources of Information in the United Kingdom* (6th edition) (London: Aslib, 1990), M. I. William *A Directory of Rare Books and Special Collections in the United Kingdom and Republic of Ireland* (London: Library Association, 1985) and R. B. Down *British and Irish Library Resources: A Bibliographical Guide* (London: Mansell,1981) and scrutinising their contents. Also of possible value are J. Burkett *Library and Information Networks in Western Europe* (London: Aslib, 1983) and *Library and Information Networks in the United Kingdom* (5th edition) (London: Aslib, 1979). Unfortunately, a large number of such directories need to be checked because few have included a comprehensive lists of special sports collections. Williams' directory, for example, lists only the special collection at Plumstead public library. Many of the large general and specialist collections have published their catalogues in hardback or microform, some of which are available for consultation in other major public and academic libraries. Two guides to published library catalogues are: R. Collison *Published Library Catalogues* (London: Mansell,1973) and B. R. Nelson *Guide to Published Library Catalogues* (Metuchen, NJ: Scarecrow Press, 1982). G. K. Hall, of New York, has published many dictionary catalogues of important collections, including the catalogues of the Applied Life Studies Library at the University of Illinois (containing considerable material on sport) and the New York Racquets and Tennis Club.

It can be a problem searching large general collections for books on highly specialised topics because of unwieldy catalogues, many of which, with subject headings of a high degree of generality, do not lend themselves to subject searching. Such difficulties are being overcome in some libraries with the development of on-line catalogues allowing searching in a number of different fields. Furthermore, it is now sometimes possible to search such catalogues on-line from remote computer terminals. From libraries with access to JANET (Joint Academic Network), for example, it is now possible to search the contents of several university library collections using the same search terms, class numbers, etc.

General library collections of special interest to the sports historian include in Britain, the British Library (for which printed author and partial subject catalogues already exist and which will shortly be available on CD-ROM (Saztec Europe and Chadwyck-Healey), allowing searches to be made using key words in the author, title, date, imprint and place of publication fields), the London Library, Plumstead and Swiss Cottage branch libraries (London), and the Mitchell Library (Glasgow).

In Canada, (27) the Metropolitan Library, Toronto, the Sports Information Resource Centre (The Canadian Coaching Association, Ottawa), the library of the University of British Columbia (Vancouver), the Leddy Library, University of Windsor (Ontario), the Weldon Library, University of Western Ontario (London, Ontario) (28) and the University of Waterloo (Waterloo, Ontario). In the United States of America, the Library of Congress, Washington DC, the Huntington Library (San Marino, California), (29) Harvard University Library (30) and the New York Public Library. (31)

Undoubtedly, there are other significant collections but these are the ones with which the author has first hand experience. A useful list of specialist sports collections in North America is included as an appendix to R. J. Higgs *Sport: A Reference Handbook* (Westport, CT: Greenwood Press, 1983), pp. 268-286. Special collections of books and periodicals on sports in general include, in Britain, the Library of the Physical Education Association of Great Britain and Northern Ireland (Sheffield Public Library) and The Sports Documentation Centre (University of Birmingham Library). Special collections of books and periodicals on individual sports, include: the Library of the Alpine Club (mountaineering, skiing and other alpine sports) (presently without a home); the BP Library of Motoring, Beaulieu (motor racing); the Kenneth Ritchie Memorial Library, Wimbledon (lawn tennis); the Library of the Cricket Society (London), the Library of Marylebone Cricket Club (London); the Horse and Hound Library at the National Equestrian Centre at Stoneleigh (equestrian sports); the National Centre for Athletics Literature, University of Birmingham Library; the Library of the Cruising Association, London; the Library of the Fly Fisher's Club, London; the Library of Rugby League, Leeds; the Library of Manchester Mountaineering Club, John Rylands University Library, Manchester, the Library of the Fell and Rock Climbing Club, University of Lancaster Library; the Library of the Rugby Football Union, Twickenham and the Library of the Royal and Ancient Golf Club, St. Andrews. In addition, several public libraries have large or special sports collections, often linked to local events or popular activities. The Picton Library in Liverpool, for example, has a large collection of works on the Grand National Steeplechase, the Central Library in Melton Mowbray has a special collection on fox-hunting. The public libraries in Chippenham and Mitcham both have large collections of books and periodicals on cricket. Sheffield Public Library which recently announced its intention to establish a Sports Library and Information Centre plans to build a special collection of mountaineering literature to supplement the Alan Rouse collection which it has recently inherited. The John Rylands University Library Manchester, houses the Brockbank Cricket Collection, the library of the Manchester Mountaineering Club and many other works of interest to the sports historian. (32) Finally, mention is made on p. 76 of the Library of the London Sports Medicine Institute.

In the United States of America; general sports collections include the International Sports and Games Research Collection, University of Notre Dame Library and the Life Sciences Library of the University of Illinois at Urbana/Champaign. (33) There are literally hundreds specialising in individual sport such as the library of the Tennis and Racquets Club, New York. (34) All British collections are listed in R. W. Cox (1991). Useful directories of American sports libraries, in addition to the general guides listed above, are: G. Lewis and G. Redmond *Sporting Heritage - A Guide To Halls of Fame, Special Collections and Museums in the United States and Canada* (Brunswick, NJ: A. S. Barnes, 1973) and P. Sodberg and H. Washington *The Big Book of Halls of Fame in the United States and Canada* (New York: R. R. Bowker, 1977). A more general, but useful international guide is J. C. Knoop and G. S. Kenyon *International Directory of Leisure Information Resource Centres* (Waterloo, Ontario: Otium Publications, 1980).

A number of bibliographies of sports books, not based on specific sports or collections have also been published. These include: E. R. Gee *Early American Sporting Books, 1734-1844* (Reprint) (New York: Haskell House, 1971); J. C. Phillips *A Bibliography of American Sporting Books* (Ann Arbor, MI: Gryphon Books, 1971); R. W. Henderson *Early American Sport - A Check List of Books by American and Foreign Authors Published in America Prior to 1860* (3rd edition) (Rutherford, NJ: Farleigh Dickinson University Press, 1977) and C. M. Van Stockum *Sport - An Attempt at a Bibliography of Books and Periodicals Published during 1890-1912 in Great Britain, United States, France, Germany, Austria, Holland, Belgium and Switzerland* (New York: Dodd and Livingston, 1914).

The recent output of monograph publications on the history of sport and other subjects of interest may be identified using *Cumulative Book Index* (an international author/subject/title index of books published in the English language since 1928, published quarterly with yearly accumulations by H. W. Wilson);

British Books in Print and the national bibliographies of appropriate nations. The latter may be identified using B. L. Bell *Annotated Guide to Current National Bibliographies* (Alexandria, VA: Chadwyck-Healey, 1986), although it should be appreciated that these vary in coverage. Whilst the *British National Bibliography*, for example, attempts officially to list all works published in Britain, the *New Zealand National Bibliography* also includes material published abroad about New Zealand. The *British National Bibliography* is published weekly, with monthly, quarterly and annual cumulative volumes. Entries are listed in the main section by class number using the Dewey Decimal System. *BNB* is also available on CD-ROM (via Chadwyck-Healey) and on-line via *BLAISE*. A cumulation of the years 1950 to 1984 is also available on microfiche. Other reference works documenting recently published and forthcoming monographs include for British books: the *Bookseller* (London: Whitaker, 1958 to date) containing an author and title list that cumulates into Whitaker's *Book of the Month and Books to Come*. These titles also appear in a classified arrangement in Whitaker's *Classified Monthly Book List* which is collated annually to form *Whitaker's Booklist*. Since 1988 Whitaker have offered a *Bookbank CD-ROM* service which includes all British books in print, forthcoming titles and provisional titles. For the United States, *Publisher's Weekly* (New York: Bowker, 1872 to date) announces new books, as does *Subject Guide to Forthcoming Books* (New York: Bowker, 1967 to date). These are prepared essentially for the book trade but provide useful 'up-to-the-minute' information for the researcher. Details of similar works for other parts of the world can be found in Sheehy.

Abstracts of a selection of scholarly history monographs are included in *Historical Abstracts* (published by Clio Press, Santa Barbara, CA since 1952), details of a selection of scholarly sports books indexed in *Sports Search*, and *Sport and Leisure* (see p. 19). Highly selective lists of scholarly monographs specifically on sports history are included in details of the NASSH Congress Book Display published in the *NASSH Proceedings*, "Recent Publications by Members' published in the ISHPES *Bulletin* (since 1972) and "Book News' published occasionally in *The Journal of Sport History* (since 1974).

Also useful for up-to-date information of recent and forthcoming publications are publishers' and booksellers' catalogues. Although academic histories of sport are published through a large number of different publishing houses, especially university presses, most popular works in Britain are published through a limited number of publishers which specialise in sports publications e.g. Pelham, Robert Hale, Willow Collins, Macdonald/Queen Anne Press, etc. Details of small run publications, such as minor club centenary booklets are more difficult to identify since many of them never find their way into indexes, bibliographies, library catalogues or even publishing records despite the fact that, if published in Britain, they should be registered with the Copyright Receipt Office of the British Library in which case they would appear in the *British National Bibliography* and copies be deposited in the British and various other national libraries. H. De Vries (Amsterdam) and Harvey Abrams (Pennsylvannia) are examples of book shops which regularly publish lists of new sports publications.

Reviews of recent publications appear in most periodicals (see list below) and are another way of getting to know what is available and an idea of their approach and worth. Reviews of some books may be traced using the periodical indexing and abstracting services outlined below. *Book Review Digest* (published quarterly by H. W. Wilson since 1905) lists and selectively abstracts reviews from popular journals and *Book Review Index* (Detroit: Gale Research Co. published bi-monthly since 1965) lists reviews in the humanities, social sciences, biography and children's literature. Although many reviews may be traced through *Book Review Index* and *Book Review Digest*, a recent review of sports coverage in these publications found that they had not kept pace with the tremendous growth of sports literature in the decade 1970-1980. Also, by the time many books are included in this type of publication, they are already a couple of years old. (35) Perhaps more useful to the sports historian is *Index to Book Reviews in the Humanities* (1960 to date) which lists reviews of both popular and scholarly books in the humanities, including history and sport.

Chapters in Books

Many important writings are published in the form of essays that are published collectively in the form of anthologies or festschriften. Although several of the bibliographies, indexing and abstracting services mentioned elsewhere in this section *(Historical Abstracts, Sports Bibliography, Sport and Leisure)* index chapters in books and festschriften, an additional source to consult is: *Essay and General Literature Index* published quarterly by H. W. Wilson since 1934. This publication indexes collections of essays on all subjects, and is particularly strong in the humanities and social sciences. Entries are by subject and author in a single alphabetical list. Annual and five yearly cumulative volumes are also produced.

Although several festschriften on sports history have been published in Germany, only one British publication, which included a single item on the history of sport/leisure, was identified during compilation of the bibliography of secondary works included in R. W. Cox *Sport in Britain* (1991).

Journal Articles

Much, although by no means all, research is reported in the form of journal articles before it is published in book form. Journal articles on the history of sport have, in recent years, appeared in many different publications as diverse as: *Albion, The British Journal of Educational Studies, The British Journal of Psychology, British Studies, Cambridge Review, Church Quarterly, Economic History Review, English Historical Review, Ethnohistory, Immigrants and Minorities, Historical Reflections, History Today, Journal of Contemporary History, Journal of Educational Administration and History, Journal of Popular Culture, Journal of Social History, Harvard Studies and Notes in Philology and Literature, Labour History, London Journal, Olympic Review, Past and Present, Physical Education Review, Research Quarterly for Exercise and Sport, Sports Place, Quest, Victorian Studies, Welsh Historical Review, Western Folklore* and *Workshop History*. (36) This is in part due to the pressure on academics to publish in a diverse range of outlets across different subject areas, the lack of specialist outlets for published works until relatively recently, the multi-disciplinary nature of sport itself and the fact that it impinges upon the lives of so many, regardless of their nationality, social class, religion or any other affiliation. Current and recent periodicals of potential interest to the sports historian may be identified using general directories such as *Ulrich's International Periodical Directory* (published annually since 1932, currently by Bowker Saur. This publication which includes yearbooks as well as journals is updated with quarterly supplements and contains a useful subject guide. Volume 31 is available in hard copy, on-line, microfische and CD-ROM.) and subject specialist directories such as E. H. Boehm and L. Adolphus *Historical Periodicals: An Annotated World List of Historical and*

Related Serial Publications (Santa Barbara: Clio Press, 1986) (five vols), the latter being restricted to those indexed by *Historical Abstracts*. 'Dead periodicals' of potential interest may be identified in earlier editions and in indexes discussed on pp.32-36. A number of the guides, bibliographies and catalogues of special collections mentioned earlier, such as A. Grobani's guides to baseball and football literature (see p. 4), H. Wright and F. Lake *Bibliography of Archery* (37) and the catalogue of the Ritchie Library at Wimbledon (38), for example, include lists of periodicals, current and dead.

Periodicals dealing specifically with sports history, published in the English language include: *The Australian Society of Sports History Bulletin* (published twice a year by the ASSH since 1984); *The ISHPES (formerly HISPA) Bulletin* (published twice a year by the International Society for the History of Sport and Physical Education since 1973); *The International Journal of the History of Sport* (IJSH) (published London three times a year in May, September and December published by Frank Cass Ltd since 1988 (formerly *The British Journal of Sports History* 1984-1987); *The Sports Historian* (formerly the *British Society of Sports History Bulletin* (published annually by the BSSH since 1993); the *Canadian Journal of the History of Sport* (CJHS) (published twice a year in May and December since 1986 by the Department of Human Kinetics at the University of Windsor, Ontario - formerly *The Canadian Journal of the History of Sport and Physical Education* 1970-1986), the *Journal of Sport History* (JSH) (published three times a year in Spring, Summer and Fall by the North American Society of Sports Historians), *Sports History* (published privately since 1987, c/o P. O. Box 183, Leesbury, VA 22074, USA), *Sporting Traditions* (published three times a year since 1984 by the ASSH) and *Ludi Medi Aevi - Newsletter of the International Society for Medieval Sport* (published twice a year by Wampusongs Publishing, Eden, North Carolina since 1989).

Multi-lingual journals (in which English is one of the languages) specialising in sports history include: *Nike* (published annually by Weidmannsche Verlagsbuchhandlung since 1989) and *Stadion* (published occasionally in Cologne since 1976). *History of Physical Education and Sport Research and Studies* was a Japanese published multi-lingual UNESCO journal devoted to sports history but this ceased publication after the first four volumes (1974-76).

Whilst *IJSH, CJHS, JSH, Nike, Sporting Traditions* and *Stadion* are international, refereed academic journals containing lengthy, in-depth scholarly articles, the *Bulletins* of the ASSH and the BSSH contain news items, including details of recent and forthcoming publications, details of conferences and occasionally shorter articles on sources and preliminary findings of research. Although most of these journals are interested in and willing to publish articles on the history of sport in all societies throughout history, there is a tendency for certain journals to contain a greater number of articles relating to one particular country or continent. The *CJHS*, for example, includes more articles on the history of sport in Canada than any other journal. Similarly, the *JSH* has greater coverage of the United States of America. Only *Nike* is restricted to one particular period of history, sport in Antiquity.

The only journals devoted exclusively to the histories of individual sports are the *Footballer: The Journal of Soccer History and Statistics* (a popular journal of soccer history published quarterly since 1988 by Sports Promotions International) and *Baseball History. The Rangers Historian* is a typescript magazine specifically devoted to the history of Glasgow Rangers Football Club. Similar typescripts are associated with Celtic and Clydebank football clubs. *The Cricketer, Cricket Statistician, Cricket World* and the *Journal of the Cricket Society* regularly carry historical and biographical works alongside articles on many other aspects of cricket past and present. Historical series of particular interest to the historian in *The Cricketer* are: "Cricketers Remembered', "Memoirs', "Milestones', "Obituaries'; in *Cricket World:* "Club Histories', "First-Class Statistics', "Great Matches', "Hall of Fame'. In February, 1990, a periodical by the name of *Iron Game History* was launched by the Todd-McLean Collection, Department of Kinesiology at the University of Texas, Austin. A bi-monthly publication, this journal is devoted to '...a better understanding of physical culture'.

Locations for periodicals in Britain up to 1980 may be identified using the *British Union Catalogue of Periodicals* and more specifically for sporting periodicals, the recently published *SPRIG Union Catalogue of Sports Periodicals* (Birmingham: Sport and Recreation Information Group, 1988). *The British Union Catalogue*, unfortunately, does not have a subject index to periodicals included and the SPRIG directory lists the whereabouts of titles in only the forty participating libraries.

Most periodicals include author and title indexes to individual volumes, sometimes with three, five or ten yearly cumulative indexes which can be helpful in checking the contents of several months or years issues at a time. It must be remembered, however, that long running periodicals have changed their names and occasionally their orientations, due to different editorial policies, from time to time.

Details of articles appearing in either remote or a large number of journals may be identified using bibliographical series indexing periodicals (e.g. *Sport Search, Completed Research in Health, Physical Education, Recreation and Dance, Sport and Leisure* (formerly *Sociology and Leisure Abstracts* see pp. 11-12) and periodical indexing/abstracting services. Periodical indexes include: *Historical Abstracts, Physical Education Index* (published quarterly by Ben Oak Publishing, Cape Girardeau, Missouri since 1978); *Sport/Physical Education Index* (published quarterly by Marathon Press, New York since 1978); *Sports Documentation Monthly Bulletin* (formerly Sports Information Monthly Bulletin), published monthly with annual cumulative indexes since 1969 by the Sports Documentation Centre, University of Birmingham) and *The Sports Periodical Index* (published monthly in Ann Arbor, by National Information Systems since 1985). With the exception of *The Sports Periodical Index*, these services abstract or index only academic periodicals. This policy poses a problem for the historian needing to be informed of popular as well as academic articles. Although *The Sports Periodical Index* currently indexes one hundred and thirty popular sports magazines, these are confined almost entirely to events in the United States. Cricket which generates perhaps more literature than any other sport is not one of the eighty sports listed. Most of the popular cricket journals mentioned above have been indexed within their own pages or in those of another cricket publication. (39)

Other indexing and abstracting services of less direct interest to the sports historian, depending upon the subject and orientation of their research, are: *British Education Index* (published quarterly with annual cumulative volumes by the University of Leeds); *British Humanities Index* (published quarterly with annual cumulative volumes in London by the Library Association since 1962 - previously the *Subject Index to Periodicals*); *Current Contents* (volumes for Arts and Humanities and Social and Behavioural Sciences in particular (published weekly by Institute for Scientific Information, Philadelphia, PA, USA available online as Current Contents Search); *Education Index* (published monthly with annual cumulative editions in New York by H. W. Wilson since 1929); *ERIC Current Index to Journals in Education* (published monthly in Phoenix, AZ, by Oryx Press); *Humanities Index* (published quarterly with annual cumulative volumes in New York by H. W. Wilson since 1974) *Leisure, Recreation and Tourism Abstracts* (published quarterly with, annual cumulative volumes, in Oxford by the Commonwealth Agricultural Bureau since 1975) and *Magazine Index* (a microfilm index to over three hundred and seventy popular magazines including over thirty devoted to sport published by the Information Access Corporation of Menlo Park, CA, produced since 1977). (40)

Citation indexes are a more specialised type of periodical index. They may be used to find articles directly related to works already discovered and found to be useful. Citation indexes will lead the researcher to other articles which cite and are therefore more recent than the known articles. Of possible use to the sports historian are: *Arts and Humanities Citation Index* and *Social Sciences Citation Index* published by the Institute for Scientific Information (Philadelphia, PA). This Institute also publishes a series of periodical indexes which reproduce the contents pages to a selection of scholarly periodicals. Of particular interest to the sports historian is *Current Contents: Social and Behavioural Sciences*. Others in the series include *Current Contents: Agriculture, Education, Life Sciences, etc.* A similar index, but specifically devoted to sports periodicals called *Sports Search: Contents of Current Journals* was started by Human Kinetics (Champaign, Illinois) in 1984 but ceased publication in 1988. Sources for identifying indexing and abstracting services include: D. Henige *Serial Bibliographies and Abstracts in History: An Annotated Guide* (Westport, CT: Greenwood Press, 1986); L. A. Harzfield *Periodical Indexes in the Social Sciences and Humanities: A Subject Guide* (Metuchen, NJ: Scorecrow Press, 1979) and J. Stephen *Inventory of Abstracting and Indexing Services produced in the UK* (London: British Library, 1983).

Unfortunately, it is not usually possible to search back in time very far using most of these periodical indexes. Most have emerged in recent years and few have undertaken retrospective indexing. An exception which may prove helpful in identifying appropriate background reading (but nothing on sport in particular) is the *Combined Retrospective Index to Journals in History, 1838-1974* (eleven vols) (Arlington, VA: Carrollton Press, 1977).

Coverage of sports history material by the various indexing and abstracting services varies considerably. (41) *Completed Research in Health, Physical Education, Recreation and Dance* has a strong bias towards the medical and life sciences, *Sports Documentation Monthly Bulletin* has greater coverage of foreign language material on sports history than the other sports periodical indexes analysed but it must be remembered that there are also foreign language or multi-lingual indexing services, such as *Sportsdokumentation* which are not reviewed in this chapter. Only *Sport/Physical Education Index* and *The Sports Periodical Index* extract from popular as well as academic journals. In terms of the amount and quality of detail provided, there is also considerable variation. The most detailed abstracts are those provided in *Historical Abstracts, Sport and Leisure* and *Leisure, Recreation and Tourism Abstracts*. *Physical Education Index* does not provide abstracts and it is only since 1987 that *Sports Documentation Monthly Bulletin* has carried annotations. *Sport and Leisure* and *Leisure, Recreation and Tourism Abstracts*, also include details of certain other forms of publications including monographs, chapters in books, and theses. A problem with using less specialised indexes is that the descriptor terms included in the thesauri are less specific and therefore do not permit such detailed interrogation.

An exciting recent development is the possibility of searching across a wide range of existing data bases simultaneously and using the same terms. *Periodicals Contents Index* (Chadwyck-Healey) now allows access to millions of articles in 19th and 20th century journals including the entire contents of *Art Index, Education Index, Essay and General Literature Index, Historical Abstracts,* etc.

Two 'one-off' indexes to periodical articles on sports history are included in J. S. Dickinson *An Annotated Bibliography of Historical Writings Related to Physical Education Published in National Professional Physical Education Journals and Proceedings in North America During the Last Decade January, 1963 - December, 1972,* M.S. thesis University of Oregon, 1973 and R. Thurmond *The History of Sport and Physical Education as a Field of Study in Higher Education,* Ed.D. Dissertation, University of Oklahoma, 1976. Thurmond's dissertation contains a bibliography, with author and subject indexes, of over one thousand articles from eight professional physical education journals published in the period 1894 to 1975.

Conference Papers

Identifying conference papers poses more of a problem. Bibliographical control of proceedings from history and sports conferences is poor, perhaps due to the limited circulation of many proceedings (often to delegates or members of the organising body only) and the fact that many proceedings appear in typescript only, especially when they are small conferences, reports of research in its infancy or research reports at an early stage of their development. Others are published in full or abstract form in the journal or newsletter of the organising body. This has been the case with the proceedings of the British Society of Sports History which were published in separate volumes from 1982 to 1986 but have since appeared in the society's *Bulletin.* The British Library Document Supply Centre at Boston Spa produces an *Index to the Conference Proceedings* it receives, including details of their contents. This appears monthly with annual, five and ten cumulations. A microfiche twenty five year cumulation is available for the years 1964-1988. It is also now available on CD-ROM (quarterly) and online via BLAISE. American indexes include: *Bibliographic Guide to Conference Publications* (published annually since 1975 by G. K. Hall) and *Index to Social Science and Humanities Proceedings* (Philadelphia: Institute for Scientific Information). An examination of their contents revealed very few items on sports history. An on-line index to conference proceedings exists but no search was carried out on this particular database in preparation of this guide.

The proceedings of the conference for the Australian Society for Sports History and abstracts of the proceedings of the North American Society of Sports Historians are published annually by the respective bodies and listed in the *HISPA Bulletin. Proceedings of the HISPA Congress* are published biannually in separate volumes and the *Proceedings of the Canadian Symposiums on Sports History* separately approximately every three years. Another sports history group occasionally publishing proceedings is the Society on the History of Sport and Physical Education in Asia and the Pacific Region. Mention has already been made of Dickinson's thesis which indexes historical writings on physical education in proceedings of select North American professional associations, as well as periodicals, between 1963 and 1972 (see above). The *HISPA* (now ISHPES) *Bulletin* reproduces the contents pages to proceedings of the majority of specialist sports history conferences and two of the bibliographical series - *Sports Bibliography, Sport and Leisure* (see p. 11) index selected conference proceedings.

Proceedings of general sports conferences usually containing papers of a historical nature include the proceedings of The Olympic Scientific Congress (published every four years by the organising committee), The International Olympic Academy (published annually), The International Council on Health, Physical Education and Recreation (published approximately every two years), The Commonwealth Conference on Sport, Physical Education, Recreation and Dance (published every four years by the organising committee), The Association for the Anthropological Study of Play (published annually), The National College Physical Education Associations (USA) (published annually) and The American Alliance on Health, Physical Education, Recreation and Dance (published annually as *Abstracts of Research Papers of the AAPHERD Convention*). All conference papers on the history of sport in Britain published before 31/12/88 are included in R. W. Cox *Sport in Britain* (1991) and updated in the *British Society of Sports History Bulletin* (1988-92), *The Sports Historian* (1993-).

Many papers presented at conferences appear, in modified form, as journal articles or chapters in anthologies at a later date, so it is important to check whether more recent and developed reports of the same research have appeared in print.

Theses

Theses on the history of sport can be a valuable source of information, especially for the academic historian, and are generally well indexed. Once again, it is necessary to check indexes under several different headings such as education, geography, history, physical education, sociology, sports science and any other subject area in which a thesis relating to the history of sport may be included. Often, two theses on the same subject (albeit with a slightly different perspective) will appear under different subject divisions within the same index because they were submitted to different academic departments. British theses accepted for higher degrees are listed in R. Bilboul *Retrospective Index to Theses of Great Britain and Ireland, 1716-1950* (Metuchen, NJ: Scarecrow Press 1975-77) and those completed since 1951 in the annual *Aslib Index to Theses Accepted for Higher Degrees in the Universities of Great Britain and Ireland* (London: Aslib, 1951, onwards). In 1987, this index modified its title to *Index to Theses Accepted for Higher Degrees by Universities of Great Britain and Ireland and the Council for National Academic Awards*, included abstracts for the first time and is now published quarterly. Such abstracts help the researcher determine the contents and methods of the theses and are therefore useful in deciding whether to consult them or not. This may save an unnecessary journey or inter-library loan request.

Indexes to historical theses in general (which sometimes include theses on the history of sport although usually only those submitted to departments of history), include: W. F. Kuehl *Dissertations on History: An Index to Dissertations Completed in History Departments of United States and Canadian Universities 1873-1960* (Lexington, KT: University of Kentucky Press, 1965) (and supplements 1960-70, 1970-1980; Santa Barbara, CA: Clio Press, 1975 and 1985); P. Bell *Dissertations on British History 1815-1914: An Index to British and American Theses* (Metuchen, NJ: Scarecrow Press, 1976); P. M. Jacobs *History Theses, 1901-70* (London: University of London Institute of Historical Research, 1976) and J. M. Horn *Historical Theses, 1971-80* (London: University of London Institute of Historical Research, 1984). The latter two publications which list only British theses are updated annually by the list of *Theses Completed* compiled and published by the University of London Institute of Historical Research. A more selective bibliography of historical theses (containing a small number on the history of sport) is V. F. Gilbert *Labour and Social History Theses* (London: Mansell, 1982).

American and certain Canadian doctoral dissertations submitted since the period covered by Kuehl can be identified by consulting one or more of the following reference sources. *Comprehensive Dissertation Index* (Ann Arbor, MI: Xerox University Microfilms). This is a computer generated index arranged by key words with an author index which attempts to list all dissertations accepted at universities of the United States. Numerous Canadian and other foreign universities have been included since 1969, but no claim is made for comprehensive coverage outside of the United States. Volumes currently exist for the years 1861-1972, 1973-1982, 1983-1987 and 1988. Abstracts of dissertations and theses are included in: *Dissertation Abstracts International* (published monthly in Ann Arbor by Xerox University Microfilms) for doctoral dissertations and *Masters Abstracts* (also published monthly by Xerox University Microfilms) for Masters theses. Dissertation Abstracts is also available for searching on-line and on CD-ROM. University Microfilms International also publishes from time to time, free *Select Lists of Dissertations Recently Submitted to North American Universities*. Although compiled primarily to advertise dissertations available for purchase from the company, they do provide a useful guide to recent dissertations. So far, separate lists of interest to the sports historian include: *Sport and Physical Education, Ancient History* and *Modern History*. A number of countries include details of theses in their national bibliographies. This is a common practice in many of the Scandinavian countries.

Many of the above guides are reviewed in M. M. Reynolds *Guide to Theses and Dissertations: An International Annotated Bibliography of Bibliographies* (Phoenix, AZ: Oryx Press, 1986). Select bibliographies of British theses and dissertations on sport, physical education and recreation which include a significant number of historical theses include: R. F. Guy "Preliminary Listing of Theses on Sport, Physical Education and Recreation Presented in British Universities in the Period 1950/ 1 - 1973/4', *Physical Education Review* 3, 2 (1980), 146-167; J. S. Keighley *PERDAS 1950-1980: A List of Theses, Dissertations and Projects on Physical Education, Recreation, Dance, Athletics and Sport Presented to UK Universities* (London: Librarians of Institutes and Schools of Education, 1981). Select lists of American theses and dissertations on sport (those submitted to Universities covered by the index) are included in *Completed Research in Health, Physical Education, Recreation and Dance* (Reston, VA: AAHPERD) published annually since 1959 and the lists of theses published in microform by the University of Oregon School of Health, Physical Education and Recreation. Select bibliographies of theses on the history of sport include: D. Abernarthy "Bibliography of Masters and Doctoral Studies Related to the History of Physical Education in the United States of America'; M. Adelman "Bibliography of Masters and Doctoral Studies Related to the History of Sport and Athletics in the United States of America' both published in E. F. Zeigler, M. L. Howell and M. Trekell *Research in the History, Philosophy and International Aspects of Physical Education and Sport: Bibliographies and Techniques* (Champaign, IL: Stipes Pub. Co., 1971). R. Thurmond's thesis (see p. 21) also contains a bibliography, with author and subject indexes, of over 1,500 masters theses and doctoral dissertations on the history of sport and physical education submitted to American universities between 1927 and 1975. Other lists of theses include: R. W. Cox *Theses and Dissertations on the History of Sport, Physical*

Education and Recreation Accepted for Higher Degrees and Advanced Diplomas in British Universities, 1900-1981 (Liverpool: Bibliographical Centre for the History of Sport, 1982); *American Theses on the History of British Sport, Physical Education and Recreation* (Liverpool: Bibliographical Centre for the History of Sport and Physical Education, 1982); B. T. P. Mutimer *Canadian Graduating Essays, Theses and Dissertations Relating to the History and Philosophy of Sport, Physical Education and Recreation* (Trois Rivieres: CAHPER - History of Sport and Physical Activities Committee, 1975) and G. Redmond "Studies of the History of Physical Education and Sport', *Bulletin of Physical Education*, X, 2 (April, 1974), 51-53. Unfortunately, all these bibliographies are now considerably out-of-date, especially bearing in mind that in recent years there has been an increased output of theses on the history of sport and recreation. In order to update these lists it will be necessary to consult recent editions of the more general indexes to theses outlined above. A very small proportion of sports history theses are listed in *The Journal of Sport History, The Sports Historian* and are abstracted and reviewed occasionally in the *International Journal of the History of Sport* and the *Journal of Sport History*.

Mention has been made of FLA theses elsewhere (see p.13 and p. 55). A small number of masters' dissertations and theses of interest to the sports historian were located in lists of theses and dissertations submitted for higher degrees in specific schools of librarianship and information studies. All types of such theses relating to the history of sport in Britain are included in R. W. Cox (1991).

An important point to realise is that theses and dissertations vary immensely in size and in content in terms of both scope and scholarship. The term thesis in North America generally refers to research reports submitted for the Master's degree. In Britain, it may refer to a report submitted for either the Master's or the Doctoral degree. Similarly, whereas the term dissertation is generally used for the Doctoral degree in North America, in Britain it is generally used to denote a research report submitted in only partial fulfilment of a degree. In some British universities, the research report submitted, may constitute one third, one half or the total requirements of the Master's degree. Doctoral theses in Britain usually constitute the total requirements of the degree although this is not always the case. In North America, Doctoral dissertations are more likely to constitute only partial requirement of the degree following one or more years of course work. Whereas British Doctoral degrees, no matter what their title - Ph.D., D.Phil. etc. are meant to be of a similar minimal standard, in North America, the structure and requirements of the Ph.D. and other Doctoral degrees such as Ed.D., D.Phys.Educ., etc. can be quite different. Masters' degrees may also vary both in Britain and in North America. M.A. degrees awarded by the Universities of Oxford and Cambridge are not post-graduate research qualifications. The M.Phil. and M.Litt. thesis in Britain is usually the report of a substantial research degree beyond the scope of the M.A. or M.Sc. degree, although there are exceptions once again in that at the Universities of Oxford and Cambridge they are usually awarded following a one year taught course for which a thesis or dissertation is not required. It is also important to note that not all Bachelor degrees in Britain are undergraduate qualifications. The B.Ed. degree in some Scottish universities is a post-graduate degree and in England so too are the B.Litt. and B.Phil. degrees.

Bibliographical control of undergraduate dissertations, Masters' dissertations (as opposed to theses) and Advanced Diplomas rarely extends beyond the scope of the individual institution to which they were submitted. This is in part due to the fact that they are usually limited in scope and not made available for consultation. Nevertheless, the libraries or departments of institutions supporting research in sports history are often worth consulting and it is not unusual to find copies of undergraduate dissertations donated to the governing body, club or library of the local area that was the subject of the research.

Finally, the conditions for consulting or borrowing theses and dissertations also vary. Some universities do not allow theses to be consulted until a certain period after examination has elapsed, some allow them to be consulted on campus but not via the inter-library loan system. Some universities allow theses to be borrowed but not dissertations. While a large number of North American Doctoral dissertations are available from the British Library Document Supply Centre at Boston Spa, most are not. Availability of British theses is outlined in the (Aslib) *Index To Theses ....* mentioned above. A more general guide is D. H. Borchardt and J. D. Thowley *Guide To Availability of Theses* (2nd edition) (London: Saur, 1981). The British Library recently produced *The British Index: Index to the British Thesis Collection* (1971-87) held in the British Library Document Supply Centre and London University (Godstone: British Thesis Service, 1988) which is helpful in determining whether a copy of a required thesis can be found within these two locations.

Current Research

Details of current research, especially non-degree work, is not easily identified. In addition to some of the bibliographical series listed on pp. 8-13 which include details of current research (e.g. *Local History News, Oral History, Urban History Yearbook* etc.), the British Library periodically publishes *Current Research in Britain* (3rd edition 1988/9) (also available on-line) and the Sports Council publish a *Guide to Ongoing Research* irregularly and even less frequently. The British Library publication lists research projects by members of staff within individual departments of institutions of higher education and several other research organisations. Although well indexed, with useful cross referencing, it does not list the research activities of postgraduate students and several of the leads the author has followed up in the past have proved to be disappointing. This is because some of the research projects turned out to be nothing more than the expressed intentions of individual academics and the work had never got underway in any serious manner. A useful indication of the status and state of the research is to look to see if anyone is funding the research and whether any reports/papers have resulted from the work to date. In the Humanities section of the 1989 (4th edition) of *Current Research in Britain*, only one sports history project is reported although many more are known by the author to be in progress. Similar problems relate to the Sports Council publication with the additional problem that it lags even further behind. Some of the research funding bodies such as the Economic and Social Science Research Council publish a newsletter which includes outline details of major research projects they are supporting and a number of universities publish details of ongoing research, lists of publications of members of staff, etc. within their annual reports or as separate lists. A further method of discovering projects in progress is to scan recent conference proceedings and to look up names of pertinent individuals and institutions and contact them directly. By using Citation Indexes (see p. 13), it may be possible to trace works by the same author and/or works citing the known author's works.

In terms of postgraduate research, the University of London's Institute of Historical Research publishes an *Annual Bibliography of Theses in Progress* and the Canadian Historical Association publishes a *Register of Postgraduate Dissertations in Progress in History and Related Subjects* annually (1966 onwards). Unfortunately, both these lists are largely restricted to theses for higher degrees registered in departments of history although a few from departments of education, geography and sociology are included.

Details of research outside institutions of higher education (academic and non-academic) is very difficult to detect. Information is sometimes gleaned from library or record office staff who are familiar with the work of visitors to their collections or by consulting the visitor's book which often asks the researcher to identify their topic of research.

D. Booker *Directory of Scholars Identifying With the History of Sport* (see p. 13) lists current research activities of most of the individuals included. So far it has been published approximately every three years since 1978.

Publications in Microform and Machine Readable Forms

At various points in this guide, reference is made to microform publications. Sometimes these are microfilmed copies of books, journals, theses, manuscripts or indexes, etc. While some of these are publications devoted solely to reproducing primary source material, they are in some senses secondary publications and are therefore discussed briefly here.

A useful source for details of microfilm, microfiche publications is the *Guide to Microforms in Print* published annually by Saur. More specialist but very useful for the historian is D. J. Munro *Microforms for Historians A Finding List of Research Collections in London Libraries* (London: University of London's Institute of Historical Research, 1990). This work is currently being expanded and updated and should be completed by the end of 1993. Specifically concerned with sport is *Health, Physical Education and Recreation Microform Publications Bulletin* which lists theses, monographs, periodicals recently made available in microform. This information is also available on Sports Discus (see p. 11).

Increasingly, CD-ROM technology is being used to communicate information. Guides to CD-ROM products are J. Mitchell*The CD-ROM Directory* (TFPL Publications) and *CD-ROMs in Print* (Meckler). Both are published annually although CD-ROM versions of both products are available and these are updated twice a year (January and June). A recent review of the two products in the *EP Journal* (July 1993) estimated an overlap of approximately 60%. A further review reported in *Inform* (November, 1993) suggested that the TFPL directory had the edge both in terms of usefulness of indexing terms and currency of information. Perhaps more useful to know for gathering up-to-date information in this rapidly evolving area are the addresses of the main vendors/suppliers. Chadwyck-Healey Ltd, Cambridge Place, Cambridge, CB2 1NR, Tel: 0223-311479; Bowker Saur, 60 Grosvenor Street, London, W1X 9DA, Tel: 071-493-5841 and Meckler Ltd, Artillery House, Artillery Row, London, SW1P 1RT, Tel: 071-796-0405. Gale Research publish a *Directory of Online Databases*. Volume 1 covers 'remote' databases and Volume 2 'Portable' databases (the kind that are available on floppy disk). Perhaps best known and more widely available is J. L. Hall and J. Brown *Online Bibliographical Databases: An International Directory* (London, Aslib).

Part III - Primary Sources

To identify primary source materials and to help make the best use of them, a number of useful guides have been published over the years. These include: J. J. Bagley *Historical Interpretations (Vol. 1 - Sources for Medieval History, 1066-1540, Vol. 2 - 1540 to the Present Day)(Newton Abbot, David and Charles, 1965)*, *The Sources of History: Studies in the Uses of Historical Evidence Series* volumes of which include: M. Crawford *Ancient History*; A. D. Mamigliano *Ancient Greece and Rome*; G. R. Elton *England 1200-1640*; C. L. Mowat *Great Britain Since 1914*; W. B. Stephens *Sources for English Local History* (2nd edition) (Cambridge: Cambridge University Press, 1981). Rather old, but perhaps still worth a separate mention is C. Gross *The Sources and Literature of English History from the Earliest Times to about 485* (London: Longmans, 1900). Also helpful for identifying and discussing the merits of specialist primary sources are the Historical Association *Helps* series and Short Guides published in *History* during the 1960s and *Great Britain 1780-1950 - Sources and Historiography* (Units 1 and 2 of the Open University course A401). Although none of these works specifically discuss sources for the history of sport, nationally or within the regions, they are useful in identifying important material for painting the historical backcloth against which analysis might take place. The only guides to sources for the history of sport so far published have been devoted to sport in the ancient world and are listed on p. 31.

Several recent histories of sport have appended notes on sources which provide a useful insight into the range of sources utilized. A fine example is S. G. Jones *Sport, Politics and the Working Class: Organised Labour and Sport in Inter-War Britain* (Manchester, Manchester University Press, 1988). One or two short articles have also been published separately. An example is B. Spear "The Use of Illuminated Manuscripts in the Study of Sports History', in G. Curl (ed.), *The Heritage of Sports, Games and Dance: Reciprocal Influences Between Great Britain and Northern Ireland and Other Countries*, Proceedings of the VI HISPA Congress, Dartford (April, 1977), pp. 572-575.

In the section which follows different forms of primary sources are discussed in terms of their potential value to the sports historian. Special problems, if any, associated with these sources in terms of accuracy and interpretation, are outlined. Bibliographical sources available for their detection or location are identified. Discussion of several different types of source material may be included under more than one heading. No separate section is devoted to diaries as a source material, for example, but they are discussed as part of the sections headed Manuscripts and Biographical Studies.

Manuscript Sources

The most important source for listings and locations of manuscript collections in the UK is the National Register of Archives (NRA), Quality House, Quality Court, Chancery Lane, London, WC2A 1HP. This body, created by the Government in 1945 as part of the Royal Commission on Historical Manuscripts, is the central collecting point for information about manuscript sources for British history outside the public records. The core of NRA consists of unpublished lists and catalogues, now numbering over 35,500 sent in by libraries, archives, museums and other bodies in this country and abroad. Not only these lists but published guides and surveys and any other available sources of information are trawled for the three indexes to the NRA: the personal index, the subject index and the companies index. All three contain information of relevance to sports history. The personal index notes papers of over 30,000 individuals. The subject index is arranged archivally rather than thematically, comprising references to the institutions which generate records rather than the places and events to which records relate. One of the thirty sections of the index is devoted to societies and associations and has a sub-head devoted to sports and recreational societies. The business index notes the records of over 16,000 British firms sub-divided according to their areas of business activity. Each reference on all three indexes provides a brief description of the papers concerned, with covering dates, location and the source of this information.

In 1987, the Commission embarked on the major task of computerising the indexes. The completion of this project, which can be expected within the next year or two, will provide researchers with two main benefits. The first will be to permit more sophisticated searches of the indexes according to date, location and the various classes and sub-classes described above. The second will be to provide as soon as practicable remote access to the indexes, mostly by networking or CD-ROM. The indexes should then be directly accessible to researchers through libraries and JANET outside London. The Royal Commission on Historical Manuscripts *Accessions to Repositories and Reports Added to the National Register of Archives* published annually by HMSO, is a useful source for keeping up-to-date with what records have recently been deposited and as the title states, reports added to the NRA Details of addresses, telephone numbers, opening hours, archivists, facilities such as photocopying etc. of record offices and libraries where provision is made for regular use by researchers are included in the Royal Commission *Record Repositories in Great Britain* (8th edition) (London: HMSO, 1987). A further useful guide is J. Foster and J. Shephard *British Archives: A Guide to Archive Resources in the UK* (2nd edition) (London: Macmillan, 1989). This publication includes many small and private collections not mentioned in the NRA's guide. These include many schools, universities, clubs and associations regardless of whether they are registered with the NRA, professionally staffed, or not, etc. It contains a useful "Guide to Key Subjects'. This lists three special collections devoted to sport and thirteen others with an interest in, or substantial volume of material on the subject. Finding aids and catalogues to individual collections have been prepared by many record offices and copies of many of these are held in the NRA Such guides can be most helpful in identifying whether a collection is likely to contain any items of interest although the point made below that sporting records are often hidden or disguised is worth bearing in mind. Mention should also be made of the *National Inventory of Documentary Sources in the United Kingdom* (Cambridge: Chadwyck-Healey, 1987 onwards), a microfiche collection of published and unpublished finding aids county record offices, public libraries and specialist repositories included in the scheme. Although a very ambitious and potentially useful project, using the system demands considerable patience because of the many referals from one fiche to another in terms of tracing the precise information required. This problem should be largely overcome with the launch of the CD-ROM version of the database in 1993. So far, the amount of material on sport included is relatively small. Perhaps this is because the collections which have so far been included in the project are not those with a great deal of material on sport. A more specialist guide is R. C. Alston *Handlist of Unpublished Finding Aids to the London Collections of the British Library* (London: British Library, 1991).

Catalogues to the manuscript holdings of individual centres have also been compiled. P. Hepworth

Archives and Manuscripts in Libraries (London: The Library Association, 1964), lists printed catalogues to a large number of British libraries and county record offices, although this is now considerably out-of-date. One of the most comprehensive and almost certainly most accessible collection of such catalogues outside the National Register of Archives is at the Library of the University of London's Institute of Historical Research (Senate House, Malet Street, London WC1E 7HU, Tel: 071-636-0272). The published catalogues of the manuscripts in the British Library are summarised in A. E. Nickson *The British Library: Guide to Catalogues and Indexes of the Department of Manuscripts* (London: British Library, 1982). These catalogues have also been revamped in a series by the publishers Chadwyck-Healey. They have consolidated the indexes to over thirty separate catalogues into one alphabetical sequence under the title *Index of Manuscripts in the British Library* (Cambridge: Chadwyck-Healey, 1984). Perhaps the most notable indexes of manuscripts in a collection are the Lists and Indexes to the Public Record Office collections. These indexes list many of the single items contained within individual files and are an excellent aid to the researcher, saving what might be otherwise hours of unfruitful searching through hundreds of different files. Recently under the title *Kew Lists* (London, HMSO, 1988) these have been published in microform (three thousand, five hundred separate fiches). The Centre for Urban and Regional Studies at the University of Birmingham, in conjunction with the Institute for Agricultural History at the University of Reading, has compiled indexes to the records of several organisations, directly or loosely associated with planning in the rural environment. Of potential interest to the sports historian are indexes to the records of the Rambling Association, The Youth Hostel Association, the Cyclist Touring Association and the British Field Sports Society. Several indexes to specific forms of manuscripts exist such as J. S. Batts *British Manuscript Diaries of the 19th Century* (Totowa, NJ: Roman and Littlefield, 1976). Even more specialised are the indexes to the private *Papers of British Cabinet Ministers, 1782-1900* prepared and published by the Royal Commission on Historical Manuscripts. These lists identify papers found in private hands, in public libraries and in record offices.

Individual manuscripts specifically concerned with sport contained within all public and many private collections are listed and indexed in R. W. Cox *Sporting Manuscripts in the UK* (1994). It is important for the sports historian to appreciate that sporting manuscripts are not only to be found in the records of sporting organisations. Many are scattered amongst more general collections. Manuscripts relating to sport (in the form of diaries, leases, notebooks, accounts, etc.) are sometimes found in the private papers of individuals, in the records of central and local government departments, the church, schools, colleges, universities, solicitors, trade unions, businesses, many with no obvious connection with sport. An account of real tennis, for example, is to be found in Samuel Pepys' diary for 2/9/1667. Information relating to the early days of many professional football clubs is to be found in the records of the church with which they were once affiliated. Many further examples are to be found in R. W. Cox (1994). From this rich and diverse range of manuscript material it is possible to learn much about the cost and nature of middle-class sporting activities. Unfortunately, there are far fewer documents of this nature prior to the twentieth century which tell us anything about the sporting activities of the poor.

It is worth noting that appointments and sometimes permission are required before certain documents can be consulted. This is especially the case in busy record offices or where large volumes of the collection are stored at remote repositories and where the documents required are particularly sensitive. Certain documents may not be available until after a certain period of time has elapsed. The documents contained within the Public Record Office are not available until after thirty years have elapsed after their production.

Some sporting organisations have their own collections of manuscripts which they themselves house and administer. These vary in scope, accessibility, facilities and the extent to which their collections have been catalogued. The MCC, for example, employ their own professional archivist whilst certain other governing bodies of sport have little more than a pile of unsorted documents in a dusty basement or loft. The value of such material varies immensely. The minute books and accounts of one organisation can be very revealing, whilst for another they contain little information of value to anyone. They may be hand written documents and therefore more difficult to read. They may be consistent in detail and format or forever changing in detail. C. P. Korr *History of West Ham United* (London: Duckworth, 1986) makes extensive use of the Club's Board minutes but it is perhaps worth stressing that many sporting organisations are very sensitive about revealing information of any form, for a variety of reasons. (42) *Archives* - The Journal of the British Records Association frequently publishes articles on manuscript collections and reviews of published catalogues, guides and finding aids which may occasionally be of interest to the sports historian. A recent paper by S. E. A. Green, (Archivist to the MCC), for example, discusses early cricket records (80, (October, 1988), 187-198).

For researchers interested in tracing the spread of sport from Britain overseas the United States General Services Administration National Archive and Record Service produce a *Directory of Archive and Manuscript Repositories in the United States* (2nd edition, New York: Oryx, 1988) and *Archives Accessions Annual*, a title and subject index to the accessions of over four thousand, five hundred archives in the United States (London: Meckler).

The Library of Congress also produces a *Union Catalogue of Manuscript Collections*. Similar types of publication exist for many other countries. Historians of sport in Canada are advised to read T. Nesmiths "Sources for the History of Sport at the Public Archives of Canada' in R. Day and P. Lindsay *Sport History Research Methodology*, Proceedings of a Workshop held at the University of Alberta (May/June, 1980), pp. 46-50.

Published Collections of Documents and Manuscripts

Finally, important and sometimes rare or inaccessible historical documents (published and manuscript) are reproduced in published compilations. These may be documents from a single collection or sometimes from different collections but relating to a common subject or theme, sometimes a combination of the two. One of the best known series is *English Historical Documents* published by Methuen. Each volume claims to provide a comprehensive corpus of evidence relating to the period under review. Volumes published to date are: Vol. I *500-1042* (compiled by D. Whitelock); Vol. II *1042-1189* (D. C. Douglas and H. Greenaway), Vol. III *1189-1327* (H. Rothwell); IV *1327-1485* (A. R. Myers); Vol. V *1485-1558*; Vol. VI *1558-1603* (D. Price); Vol. VII (i) *1603-1640* (I. Roots), (ii) *1640-1660* (I. Roots); Vol. VIII *1660-1714* (A. Browning); Vol. IX *American Colonial Documents to 1776* (M. Jensen); Vol. X *1714-1783* (D. B. Horn); Vol. XI *1783-1832* (A. Aspinall and

E. A. Smith); Vol. XII (i) *1833-1874* (G. M. Young and W. D. Hancock), (ii) *1874-1914* (W. D. Hancock). Several volumes contain information of considerable interest to the sports historian. By way of example, Vol. II contains William Fitzstephen's biography of Thomas of Canterbury which is very illuminating of popular pastimes. Vol. VIII has a section devoted to "Sport, Tragedy and Crime' (pp. 504-512).

In recent years, Harvester Press (now part of Research Publications) has produced a valuable collection of documents on microfilm under the title *The Condition of England, 1800-1900*. Vol.umes in the series include: *The Victorian City, Industrialisation and Social Reform: The Papers of Sir Edwin Chadwick* with several more in preparation. Smaller compilations that are more likely to interest the social historian, including the sports historian researching the background to a set of events are R. C. Richardson and T. B. James *The Urban Experience: A Source Book* (Manchester: Manchester University Press, 1986) and the more general *English Life Series* (London: Batsford) and *Human Documents Series* edited by E. R. Pike (London: Allen Unwin), both published in the 1960s.

Specifically relating to sport are: S. G. Miller *Arete - Ancient Writings, Papyri, and Inscriptions on the History and Ideals of Greek Athletics and Games* (2nd edition) (Berkeley, CA: University of California Press, 1990), R. S. Robinson *Sources for the History of Greek Athletics* (Cincinatti: The Author, 1951), W. E. Sweet *Sport and Recreation in Ancient Greece: A Source Book* (London: Oxford University Press, 1987) and W. Decker *Some Documents on Sport and Physical Education in Ancient Egypt* (Sankt Augustin: Verlag Hans Richarz, 1978). The International Council for Sport and Physical Education (ICSPE) sponsored a five volume Compilation of Sports Historical Documents (Leipzig: German College for Physical Culture) in the 1970s but these are published in languages other than English. The only such compilation relating specifically to sport in Britain is a collection of documents pertaining to the history of elementary school physical training put together by the author for publication in the *Journal of Sources in Educational History*, 4, 3 (1981).

Contemporary Monographs

Monographs providing primary evidence may be identified in much the same way as described for monographs containing secondary information although separate catalogues will need to be consulted for earlier publications (for which there are very few entries for sport) e.g. A. W. Pollard and G. R. Redgrave *A Short-Title Catalogue of English Books Printed in England, Scotland, Ireland, Wales and British America and English Books Printed In Other Countries, 1475-1640* (2nd edition) (New York: Index Committee of the Modern Language Association of America, 1972), D. Wing *Short Title Catalogue, 1641-1700* (New York: Index Committee of the Modern Language Association of America, 1972). *The Eighteenth Century Short Title Catalogue* (lists British Library holdings as at 1986, later information is available on-line) and *The Nineteenth Century Short Title Catalogue* (London: Avero Publishers Ltd 1986 to date). More useful is the *New Cambridge Bibliography of English Literature* (Cambridge: Cambridge University Press, 1981). Vols for the 18th and 19th centuries include significant sections on sport. Retrospective national bibliographies for Britain and several other countries are listed in *Retrospective National Bibliographies* compiled by M. Beaudiquez (Munich: IFLA, 1986).

Older texts are sometimes difficult to consult because few copies exist and where they do they are usually part of a reference collection and not available for inter-library loan. Facsimile productions of 'Highly important, original monographs and dissertations on modern British history' have recently been published by Garland in an eighteen volume series edited by P. Stansky and L. Hume. Several other such series have also been published. Reprints of many important and popular works such as the *Badminton Library* (43) and many cricket books (44) have been produced in recent years. Facsimile reprints of a number of important sports monographs, now out of print, have also been produced by Microform Publications (at the School of Health, Physical Education and Recreation at the University of Oregon, Eugene) and are listed in their regular *Bulletins* (see p. 26). Many further examples are to be found in *The Eighteenth Century Guide to Microfilm Collections* (Research Publications, 1989).

As with manuscripts, it is important to remember that the titles of individual works do not necessarily reflect their sporting content. William Fitzstephen *Descriptio Noblissimae Civitatis Londoniae* (1175) and J. Stow *Survey of London* (1603) provide immensely valuable information on the popularity of sport in London during Medieval times and in the Middle Ages, but someone scanning through the library catalogue may not even consider consulting such works for evidence of sport.

Examples of anthologies of literature on sport collecting the works of one or more authors related to a specific theme include A. Dent *World of Shakespeare: Sports and Pastimes* (Reading: Osprey, 1973) and M. Vale *The Gentleman's Recreations - Accomplishments and Pastimes of the Englishmen, 1580-1630* (Studies in Elizabethan and Renaissance Culture Series No 1) (Cambridge: D. S. Brewer, 1977). The Bible has been cited by a number of sports historians, an index to references to sport in the Old Testament has been compiled by G. Eisen. (45)

Sources of monographs not to be overlooked by the enthusiastic researcher are private collectors and dealers. During the past few decades, collecting antiquarian sports books has become a popular hobby, if not investment, for a significant number of individuals. Collectors may occasionally allow the serious researcher to consult items of interest from their personal libraries. Many collectors of sports books may be identified in the *International Directory of Book Collectors* (London: Trigon Press, occasional); dealers in D. A. Hamilton *Skoob Directory of Bookshops in the United Kingdom* (2nd edition) (London: Skoob Books,1988), - a useful topographically arranged directory with name and subject indexes.

Contemporary Periodical Articles (including Newspaper reports)
(Also see Sports Journalism)

In addition to the reference sources already noted for identifying and locating periodical articles of a secondary nature, the following guides are helpful for primary material. For identifying runs of nineteenth century periodicals the researcher might usefully consult the *Waterloo Directory of Periodicals 1824-1900*. Unfortunately, this directory does not include a subject index.

For identifying the contents of individual periodical runs, W. E. Houghton *Wellesley Index to Victorian Periodicals 1824-1900* (five vols) (London: RKP, 1972-89) is one of the most useful. This publication indexes fifty prominent serials, including such titles as *Contemporary Review* and *The Gentleman's Magazine.*

Several other titles also contain articles on sport, some of them substantial and extremely valuable. This index does not, however, lend itself to subject searching since entries are arranged by periodical in chronological order. It has author, but not subject indexes. What is helpful to the user are the introductions to each of the periodicals indexed, indicating the particular religious, political or intellectual milieu with which it was associated, the personalities involved in its publication, its policy and the nature of its readership. Greenwood Press have recently produced individual indexes to selected general magazines considered by the editors to reflect contemporary concerns and opinions and providing invaluable illustrations and photographs. To date, the series includes indexes to *The Strand Magazine, Chartist Circular, New Moral World.*

Unfortunately, apart from a brief discussion of major American sporting periodicals in F. L. Mott five volume *A History of American Magazines,* there is, as yet, no directory to the many specialist sporting periodicals of the nineteenth and early twentieth centuries (many of which survived for only a few issues) nor indexes to their contents. Since many of these periodicals frequently changed their title, had limited circulation and are not held in the major library collections, a directory and union list of early sports periodicals would be of immense assistance to the sports historian.

Among the more prominent general sports periodicals are the *Badminton Magazine of Sports and Pastimes* (1895-1923); *Baily's Magazine of Sports and Pastimes* (1860-1926); *Bell's Life in London and Sporting Chronicle* (1822-1886), *Illustrated Sporting and Dramatic News* (1874-1974), and *The Field* (1853-). Details of more specialist periodicals sometimes appear in guides to the literature (e.g. A. Grobani's guides to baseball and football literature op. cit. p. 4), specialist library catalogues (e.g. *The Kenneth Ritchie Wimbledon Library Catalogue* London, 1991, lists many British and foreign periodicals on tennis), bibliographies (e.g. F. Lake and H. Wright *Bibliography of Archery* Manchester: Simon Archery Foundation, 1974, p. 324) and guides to sources contained within published histories and theses (e.g. "A Note on Sources' in D. Smith and G. Williams *Fields of Praise: The Official History of the Welsh Rugby Football Union, 1881-1981* (Cardiff: University of Wales Press, 1980) which lists many rugby union magazines). A useful introduction to the growth of the sporting press is contained in T. Mason *Sport in Britain* (London: Faber and Faber, 1988), pp. 46-52. C. B. Cone *Hounds in the Morning: Sundry Sports of Merry England* (Lexington: University of Kentucky Press, 1981) reproduces a selection of writings from *The Sporting Magazine* 1792-1836.

Of particular interest to many sports historians are newspaper articles since these often carried commentary on important events as well as publishing competition results, league tables, correspondence and adverts, etc. Amongst the first national specialist sporting newspapers were *Bell's Life in London* (1822), *The Field* (1853), *Sporting Life* (1859), *The Sportsman* (1865), *The Sporting Chronicle* (1871) and the *Athletic News* (1875). By 1900, however, several national dailies were also devoting significant attention within their pages to sport with cricket, football and athletics usually the most prominent activities. In 1937, Henry Durant did a survey of the contents of twelve daily and eleven Sunday newspapers. The daily papers devoted on average of 11.4 per cent of their total space to sport, whilst the Sunday papers averaged 17.7 per cent. According to a further survey in 1955, 46 per cent of the *Daily Mirror* and 33 per cent of the *Daily Mail* were filled by sport. (46)

Unfortunately, working with newspapers can be fraught with problems. Many were short lived whilst others changed their titles and or editorial policies from time to time. A. L. Parsons in researching his history of Durham City Cricket Club (47) found that they were the only significant source material remaining. Searching through files of newspapers was, however, a tiring, time consuming and often unrewarding occupation. Carr in his *English Fox-Hunting: A History* (48) reported the sporting press of the 19th century to be not only tedious but full of exaggerated statements. The owner of the newspaper, the audience they addressed, and the frequency with which they were published affected their contents. It was only as the Victorian age progressed that they began to widen their appeal and report upon cricket, football and other such sporting activities.

Even then, the reporting was spasmodic and dominated by seasonal clusters around Easter, Whitsuntide, wakes weeks and Christmas. Other problems identified by researchers working with newspapers are discussed in A. Metcalfe "The Use of the Newspaper in Sports History Research', *Proceedings of the VIIth HISPA Congress,* Paris (April, 1978), pp. 557-567.

The titles of a large number of sports newspapers and magazines may be identified using national directories such as *The Times Tercentenary Handlist of English and Welsh Newspapers, Magazines and Reviews* (London: The Times, 1920); directories devoted to specific regions or subjects such R. Webber *World List of National Newspapers: A National Union List of National Newspapers in the Libraries of the British Isles* (London: Butterworths, 1976); J. P. S. Ferguson *Dictionary of Scottish Newspapers* (Edinburgh: National Library of Scotland, 1984) and the Library Association *Bibliography of British Newspapers Series*; union lists such as J. W. S. Gibson *Local Newspapers, 1750-1920: England and Wales, Channel Islands and Isle of Man: A Select Location List* (London: Federation of Family History Societies, 1987) and A. R. Hewitt *Union List of Commonwealth Newspapers in London, Oxford and Cambridge* (London: University of London Institute of Commonwealth Studies, 1962) and catalogues of individual collections. By far the largest collection of newspapers in Britain and one which contains many serials (general and special) of interest to the historian of sport in modern Britain, is the British Library. Newspapers prior to 1800 are held in the main reference collection at the British Museum and all post 1800 newspapers at the British Library's Newspaper Library at Colindale Avenue, Hendon, London NW9 5HE (Tel: 081-200-5515). Approximately, two hundred and fifty titles starting with the word sport are included in the *Catalogue of the Newspaper Library* (London: British Museum Publications, 1975) but on careful examination many additionally useful titles are to be found. *Benn's Media Directory* (1978-) (previously *Newspaper Press Directory* 1948-) and *Willing's Press Guide* (1980-) between them provide annual listings of UK and some foreign newspapers and periodicals, giving details of frequency, average circulation, etc. Other reference works worthy of mention include C. Nelson *British Newspapers and Periodicals, 1641-1700: A Short List of Serials Printed in England, Scotland, Ireland and British America* (New York: Index Society, 1987) and D. Linton *The Newspaper Press in Britain: An Annotated Bibliography* (London: Mansell, 1987). *The 19th Century Short Title Catalogue* (see p. 31) includes newspapers, but not *The 18th Century Short Title Catalogue.*

Indexes to the contents of individual newspapers are relatively few. While detailed comprehensive indexes exist for *The Times* newspaper since 1790 in published form, indexes for certain other daily newspapers are recent (for example, the *Clover Newspaper Index* acts as an index to the *Daily Telegraph, Financial Times, Guardian, Observer* but has only been in existence since 1987) or do not exist at all. The *British Humanities Index* (1962 to date, formerly the *Subject Index to Periodicals* 1918-) indexes selected items from what are termed 'quality newspapers' and the *World Reporter* database gives full-text retrieval of articles from recent years of leading national papers. A separate on-line index to the contents of the *New York Times* exists which was recently analysed for its contents on sport. (49) Chadwyck-Healey have recently announced the availability of a CD-ROM index to *The Times* which cumulates all four hundred and fifty Quarterly issues of *Palmer's Index* covering the years 1790 to 1905. *The Official Index to The Times 1906-1942* also on CD-ROM will be available in due course. Recent years of *The Guardian, The Daily Telegraph, The Independent* and *The Times* have all been made available on CD-ROM (Chadwyck Healey). Some newspapers, including many local ones, maintain an in-house index which they may be willing to allow the researcher to consult or be willing to search for a fee. *The Guardian's* hand written index to the early years of the paper is now held in the Manchester Central Library. Several local studies collections hold indexes to particular newspapers or several newspapers over a specific period of time, which have been compiled by a local history group, school, adult education class or Manpower Services scheme. More often the local history librarian has maintained a clipping service, collecting and indexing articles of local interest appearing in national and local newspapers. These may be catalogued separately, or entered in the main local studies catalogue. A rather exceptional index to cricketing literature published in the Norwich newspapers is J. S. Penny *Cricketing References in Norwich Newspapers, 1701-1800* (Norwich, The Compiler, 1978). Several compilations of sports newspaper cuttings have been published in recent years, for example, *The New York Times Scrapbook Encyclopaedia of Sports History* (New York: Arno Press, late 1970s) includes volumes on baseball, basketball, boxing, American football, golf, indoor sports, horse racing, auto sports, soccer, professional hockey, track and field, water sports and winter sports. Collections of sports cuttings from British newspapers include: I. Wooldridge *Great Sporting Headlines* (London: William Collins and Sons., 1984), J. Lovesey *The Sunday Times Sports Book* (London: World Work, 1979), C. Nawrat, et. al. *The Sunday Times Chronicle of Twentieth Century Sport* (London: Hamlyn, 1992)the annual *Guardian Book of Sport*, the Unwin Hyman series of articles on individual sports from *The Observer* and *The Back Page: A Century of Newspaper Coverage* series published by Macdonald/Queen Anne Press, and for which volumes so far exist for cricket, football and horse racing. Exclusively concerned with newspaper feature articles associated with the Olympic Games is M. Brant *The Games: A Complete News History* (London: Proteus, 1980).

A recent phenomenon has been the development of 'fanzines'. Stephen Redhead has made extensive use of this source in his *Football With Attitude* (Manchester: Wordsmith, 1991). Often associated with an individual club and, so far, mainly soccer teams, these publications reflect the attitudes, usually through strip cartoons of the paying supporter. An extensive listing of fanzines, compiled by C. Harte, is to be published by the British Society of Sports History in1994.

Finally, a number of important and popular sports magazines have been reprinted to assist the historian in his work. *Bell's Life of London and Sporting Chronicle* for example, has been recently made available on microfilm and is presently being indexed by R. T. Rivington. (50) Greenwood Press has reprinted several American titles in microform such as *American Athlete* and *Cycle Trade Review, Annals of Sporting and Fancy Gazette, All Outdoors* . (51)

Unfortunately, many popular sports magazines and newspapers have been discarded by the governing bodies and libraries which produced or subscribed to them because they were not considered very important in the long term future. Perhaps this attitude is understandable in light of the fact that few sportsmen and women are usually interested in their sport beyond participating in or watching contemporary events and that most of the popular magazines and newspapers were announcements of forthcoming events and match results. Because many of the sports periodicals were published privately by the governing bodies and circulated only to members, only a small proportion of those which existed found their way into major library collections.

Directories

Alongside newspapers, commercial directories provide one of the first sources that should normally be consulted in examining the local history of modern sports. They appeared in most regions from the 18th century onwards, recording the commercial and topographical details of communities and listing the principal inhabitants and their occupations. However, they provided little information on sport until the 1860s. Thereafter, the Post Office and other directories for various towns provide potted histories of clubs, details of their facilities, membership and officials. Useful directories of directories are J. F. Norton *Guide to the National and Provincial Directories of England and Wales, Excluding London Published Before 1856* (London: The Royal Historical Society, 1950); G. Shaw and A. Tipper *British Directories Published in England and Wales* (1850-1950) and *Scotland* (1773-1950) (Leicester: Leicester University Press, 1989) and P. J. Atkins *The Directories of London, 1677-1977* (London: Mansell, 1990). A large collection of provincial directories is held in the library of the University of London Institute of Historical Research.

Parliamentary Publications and Records

Over the past century the Government has become increasingly involved in legislating on sports related issues. Although it is only since 1967 that there has been a minister with special responsibility for sport, the government has long been concerned with sport in some capacity or another, through a number of departments especially the Ministry of Defence (and its predecessors) and more recently the Department for Education and the Department of the Environment.

Government publications is a term used to cover the published material generated by Parliament and various government departments. Material prepared for MP's to assist them in their work is often referred to as parliamentary or official publications. Such publications can take many forms from single sheets of regulations to lengthy discussion documents, all of which, up to now, have been published by HMSO. Other publications, produced by government departments as a result of their work, and not expressly intended for parliamentary use, are generally referred to as non-parliamentary publications. Such publications may also take several forms but are not necessarily published by HMSO.

Hansard, and its predecessor, records debates in the Houses of Parliament and '...is a verbatim report of all that was said with discreet editing of 'slips of the tongue' and pointless repetitions...' It also includes oral and written questions and answers. Volumes of *Hansard* are admirably indexed together with a separate index volume at the end of each session. Not only the names of members speaking, but the whole range of subjects debated or touched on in questions are given. Indexes for the years 1803 to 1941 and the proceedings since the 1988/9 session are now available on CD-ROM (Chadwyck-

Healey). The *Journals* of the House of Commons (1547 onwards) and the House of Lords (1510 onwards), also provide record of what was decided (as opposed to what was said). Sections of *Hansard* dealing with sporting issues since 1967, have been reproduced for members and staff of the Sports Council, copies of which are held in the Sports Council Information Centre library.

There are, of course, many other types of parliamentary and non-parliamentary publications which may be of interest to the sports historian, including the annual and occasional reports of government departments, the reports of Royal Commissions and Select Committees. It may be necessary to trace how a particular policy was moulded at different stages of the legislative process, what was stated in the final Act and how it was implemented. More detailed discussion of the different forms of publications, including their role in the legislative process are discussed in P. and G. Ford *Guide To Parliamentary Papers: What They Are, How To Find Them, How To Use Them* (Shannon: Irish University Press, 1972) and J. Olle *An Introduction to British Government Publications* (2nd edition) (London: Association of Assistant Librarians, 1975).

Bibliographic control of HMSO publications is excellent. Daily, monthly and yearly lists are produced, the three providing detailed subject and title indexes, including, where appropriate, the names of persons responsible for producing various reports. The annual *Catalogue of UK Official Publications* covering the years since 1980 is now available on CD-ROM (Chadwyck-Healey). POLIS provides an on-line index to all of parliament's proceedings and papers and is usually available in the larger public and university libraries. Useful guides for the researcher attempting to track down and use government papers are: R. Stavely and M. Piggott *Government Information and the Research Worker* (2nd edition) (London: Library Association, 1965), M. F. Bond *Guide to the Records of Parliament* (London: HMSO, 1964), and J. Pemberton *British Official Publications* (2nd edition) (Oxford: Pergamon, 1973). Pemberton's work includes a concordance of Command Papers 1833-1972, an alphabetical list of Royal Commissions 1900-1972, and a select list of important departmental committees and inquiries 1900-1972. More recent is D. Butcher *Official Publications in Britain* (London: Library Association Publishing, 1991), and D. M. Marshall "Exploiting the Official Publications of the United Kingdom' in N. Roberts *Use of Social Science Literature* (London: Butterworths, 1977), pp. 261-285 and S. Richard *Directory of British Official Publications: A Guide to Sources* (2nd edition) (London: Mansell, 1984), the last being the first in a series initiated by the Library Association/HMSO working party. It is probably the most complete guide to British official publications to date and provides details of the various issuing bodies and the sort of material they publish. This is particularly useful for the large and increasing number of such bodies which do not publish through Her Majesty's Stationery Office. Researchers specifically interested in statistical information should consult the references mentioned on pp. 7-8.

In 1988, Chadwyck-Healey published a five volume *Subject Catalogue of the House of Commons Parliamentary Papers, 1801-1900*. This catalogue classifies the papers into one or more of nineteen major subject areas such as education, finance, industry, etc. Although sport is not included as one of the major subject divisions, several sports related topics appear as sub-headings (e.g. Recreation, Horse Racing) help locate more specific items of interest. Unfortunately, no thesaurus has been compiled to assist the researcher trace more obscure subject headings. Reference is made to the paper number, to the session, volume and volume page number for each of the references included. Unlike earlier attempts to create subject indexes this catalogue indexes all documents published in the five thousand, nine hundred volumes of House of Commons bound series between 1801 and 1900, as well as all those included only in House of Lords series and other locations: annual reports, bills, memoranda and statistics, etc.

Various facsimile reprints and compendiums of parliamentary papers have been produced over the years. These include Scholarly Resources Ltd's one hundred and forty seven volume reprint of parliamentary papers presented between 1714 and 1800, the Irish University Press one thousand volume reprint of 19th century material and P. and G. A. Ford *Breviate of Parliamentary Papers* series (three vols) (Oxford: Blackwells) (covering the years 1900-1954). These volumes contain some of the more significant parliamentary papers of the nineteenth and early twentieth centuries, a few of which may be of value to the sports historian. For example those relating to horse racing and betting. For assistance in tracing microform publications see p. 26.

Large collections of British parliamentary papers are held in several major university and public libraries. Amongst the most comprehensive collections is the Official Publications Section of the British Library. The individual ministry libraries have comprehensive collections of government documents relating to their particular area of responsibility. These are usually catalogued in more detail with helpful cross referencing and generally have a well qualified staff highly familiar with the material available. Those government department libraries containing documents of possible interest to the sports historian, depending on the subject of their investigation, include the libraries of the Department for Education, the Department of the Environment, the Ministry of Defence and the Home Office. All of these are listed in R. T. Adkins (ed.), *Guide to Government Department and Other Libraries* (28th edition) (London: British Library Science Reference and Information Service, 1988). A useful guide to certain types of information contained within Government ministry libraries is A. F. Comfort and C. Loveless *Guide to Government Data: A Survey of Unpublished Social Science Material in Libraries of Government Departments in London* (London: British Library of Political and Economic Science, 1974). Permission to use these libraries is restricted and advanced requests in writing are required as a matter of policy.

The work of parliamentary committees is recorded in extensive series of committee proceedings and of evidence books which are kept in the House of Lords Record Office in Westminster (London, SW1A OPW, Tel: 071-219-3074).

The British Library Official Publications Library and the libraries of a number of universities in Britain contain sets (of differing size) of official government documents of foreign nations. The most comprehensive collection is that contained in the library of the London School of Economics. While details of these collections may be discovered in some of the guides to subject collections listed above, it should be appreciated that the legislative processes may vary immensely from one country to another, as may their relationships with regional authorities and other bodies. Users are advised to consult guides to these collections before attempting to extract evidence from them.

Central Government Department Records

The Public Record Office holds the manuscript records of central government departments. The records of the Ministry of Education (later the Department of Education and Science, and now the Department for Education) contain a good deal of material. There are, for example, files relating to local education authority facilities for physical training and recreation under the various acts (in the class ED56); to the evening play centres which operated between the wars (ED65); to the National Fitness Council (ED113). On the public order aspects of sport, there is a good deal of material in the records of the Home Office and the Metropolitan Police. A report of the incident at Epsom Race Course during the running of the Derby on 3rd June, 1913, when suffragette Emily Davison flung herself in front of the King's horse, Anmer, at Tattenham Corner, for example, is to be found in MEPO 2 -1551, fos. 6-8. There is information on the diplomatic issues raised by sporting events (for example the 1936 Olympic Games) in the records of the Foreign Office. Direct government provision of sports facilities and training is largely confined to the armed services; there is information in the records of the War Office, Admiralty and Air Ministry. The financial implications of all this activity are dealt with in the records of the Treasury. Information relating to sport is also to be found in the records of the Ministry of Agriculture, Fisheries and Food, the Board of Trade, (see p. 72) etc. Users of the Public Records are advised to consult the official *Guide to the Contents of the Public Record Office* (three vols) (London: HMSO , 1963-68) and the *Current Guide* (London: HMSO, 1992). Part One of the *Current Guide* contains a brief history of each Government department, law court or other institution, outlining its development and functions and indicating the classes containing its records. Part Two describes the nature and content of each class of records, including their data span, the number of records and their format, nature and contents and a note of any variation from the standard thirty-year closure to public inspection. Part Three is a comprehensively cross-referenced index to parts One and Two. For details of lists and indexes to the PRO collection see p. 27-30.

Local Government Records
(Also see Regional Histories of Sport)

The records of local government may be of interest, especially to the local historian of sport. H. Meller in her *Leisure and the Changing City, 1870-1914* (London: R.K.P., 1976) makes extensive use of the reports and minutes of committees of the local Council in the City of Bristol. As with central government, it was not until recent years, mainly since Local Government reorganisation in 1974, that many authorities set up separate committees for sport and recreation. Swimming baths usually came under Baths and Wash Houses, outdoor recreation areas under Parks, Gardens and Cemeteries, indoor sport under Education. Still today, countryside recreation may come under the responsibility of a different committee from the one for indoor recreation. Some local authority facilities are provided and or managed by two separate committees or department e.g. Education and Recreation in which case relevant information may be found in the records of more than one committee. The annual reports of the local education authority School Medical Officer usually contained a report by the Organiser/ Inspector/Advisor for physical education which included sections on developments in local schools, evening play centres, school camps, etc. (See Sport and Education, pp. 68-72.)

Copies of annual reports, published minutes of the various committees, etc. are usually held in the local municipal library, unpublished documents in the local county or district record office. The format and detail contained within these documents varies immensely. Generally, it was only the large urban authorities that made special provisions for sport and recreation until recent years and therefore these are the only ones likely to include much discussion of and policy towards sports.

Contemporary Literature
(Also see History of Sports Fiction)

Several eminent sports historians have made effective use of contemporary literature as a source for illustrating or understanding contemporary values and concerns of the period under investigation. (52) Henry Newbolt *Vitae Lampada,* Thomas Hughes *Tom Brown's Schooldays* and Charles Kingsley *Westward Ho* have been cited many times in historical assessments of public school athleticism. Undoubtedly in due course Dick Francis, *High Stakes* (London: Michael Joseph, 1975), and his many other stories centred on the world of horse-racing and David Storey *The Sporting Life* (London: Longman, 1960) (an account of the harsh world of rugby league), will be used as graphic descriptions of sporting life in 1960s and 70s. It has already been pointed out earlier that in the absence of more direct sources of information for his *History of Swimming in Britain,* Orme made extensive use of literary sources, commenting that "The writers of Classical Rome, of early epic and saga, of medieval romance, Elizabethan drama and the early novel all have something to say about swimming'. (53) According to J. M. Carter in "All Work and No Play? A Review of the Literature of Medieval Sport' (*Canadian Journal of the History of Sport,* XI, 2 (December, 1980, 67-72). "Verse and prose fiction can provide us with the tone of Medieval life that no other documents can'. Among the many Medieval; classics which contain information on sport are: Gottfried of Strassburg*Tristan,* Sir Thomas Malory *Le Morte D'Arthur,* Chaucer *Canterbury Tales* and Longland *Vision of Piers and Plowman.* A. Dent *World of Shakespeare: Sports and Pastimes* (Reading: Osprey, 1973) is in fact devoted to reproducing extracts on sport in the writings of one particular author - William Shakespeare. Bibliographies of works of fiction are included on p. 71.

Anthologies of writings from selected works include: A. C. Jenkins *The Sporting Life* (London: Blackie, 1974), V. Scannel *Sporting Literature: An Anthology* (London: Oxford University Press, 1987) and L. S. Wood and H. L. Burrow *Sports and Pastimes in English Literature* (London: Thomas Nelson and Sons, 1925). More concerned with sport in North America are R. J. Higgs *Laurel and Thorn: The Athlete in American Literature* (Lexington: The University of Kentucky Press, 1981) and *The Sporting Spirit: Athletes in Literature and Life* (New York: Harcourt Brace Jovanovich, 1977).

Finally, songs as well as prose and verse are sometimes expressive of sporting events, attitudes and values and have been used by historians to good effect. (54)

Oral Evidence

It is only in relatively recent times that the recording of sound has been possible. Over the past few decades, oral recordings made of commentaries on important events, interviews with personalities, etc. have been preserved in national and local collections, the most prominent of which is the British Library's National Sound Archive at 29 Exhibition Road, South Kensington, London, SW7 2AS (Tel:

071-589-6603). Other significant collections in Britain containing information on sport include the sound archive of the Imperial War Museum in Lambeth which includes many reminiscences of sport in the Services and especially during wartime and the BBC Sound Archives at Broadcasting House, London, W1A 1AA (Tel: 071-580-4468 ext 2809).

Details of these and other collections in the UK are contained in L. Weerasinghe and J. Silver *Directory of Recorded Sound Resources in the UK* (London: British Library National Sound Archive, 1989). This may be updated to some extent by checking the announcements on "Current British Research' in each issue of *Oral History*, a periodical published in the Spring and Autumn of each year since 1972 by the Oral History Society. Unfortunately, only three entries are included under the heading of sport in the above directories. This is because it includes only specialist collections and not details of the many general collections with sports material contained within.

During the 1970s and 80s many local museums and history groups made recordings of interviews with older members of the local community in which they were asked to recall events and personalities of bygone days. Alongside work and education, sport features quite prominently, especially among male members of the community who were interviewed. Many of these recordings are now in the hands of the local museum, library, record office or local history society and may be available for consultation. Examples include Blackheath, Rotherham and West Ham Public Libraries.

In North America, where considerably more attention has been directed to oral history, large collections of material of a general and specialist nature have been established. Notable collections include the University of Columbia Oral History Collection, (55) the University of California, Berkeley, Radcliffe College (56) and several of the sporting halls of fame, details of which are included in E. Wasserman *Oral History Index: An International Directory of Oral History Interviews* (published annually by Meckler since 1990). A collection is also housed at the Australian Gallery of Sport in Melbourne which may be of interest to historians of touring MCC sides.

Where appropriate evidence does not exist (and this may become more of a problem in the future as aeroplanes, cellular mobile telephones, electronic mail, video conferencing and the like make traditional means of communicating via the written word redundant), the sports historian may decide to interview individuals himself. This may well be the case where impressions of a particular group are required and where other forms of evidence are inadequate, inaccessible or do not exist. In this instance, it is important to follow the ground rules laid down by oral historians. (57) As R. Streeton in his biographical study of P. G. H. Fender warns 'Old men's stories, like an angler's yarn, have to be treated with caution'. (58)

Unfortunately, oral evidence has not been extensively used by the sports historian in Britain to date. This is despite the publication of several articles praising its merits and describing techniques. For a fine example of how oral history techniques have been exploited by the sports historian, one is advised to read W. J. Baker's biography of Jesse Owens.(59) Helpful discussion of the value of oral history is provided in A. Seldon and J. Pappworth *By Word of Mouth: Elite Oral History* (London: Methuen, 1983) and D. Henige *Oral Historiography* (London: Longmans, 1982). A useful bibliography of literature on oral history, including a few items on sport is R. Perks *Oral History: An Annotated Bibliography* (London: The British Library, 1990).

Pictorial Records

Pictorial records often provide a unique and therefore important source of information on sport. (60) Reference has already been made of the collection of ancient Greek amphora in the British Museum depicting sporting scenes from which Classical sports historians have drawn valuable information and mention is made elsewhere of the Bayeaux Tapestry and its use as a source for Medieval sport. J. A. R. Pimlott's study of popular recreations in the *Visual History of Modern Britain Series* (London: Studio Vista, 1968) illustrates a wider range of pictorial sources from illuminated manuscripts through paintings, prints and etchings, to photographs, depicting sporting activity from the Middle Ages to modern times. For some sports historians pictorial sources are of primary concern since their interest is in the development of sport art itself. A useful general guide to film video, photographic, portrait and mixed media archive collections is G. P. Gornish *Archival Collections of Non-Book Material* (2nd Edition) (London: British Library, 1986).

Photographs

Several guides and directories have been published in recent years which are helpful in locating photographic sources of information. These include: R. Eakins *Picture Sources in the UK* (London: Macdonald, 1985), H. and M. Evans *The Picture Researchers Handbook: An International Guide to Picture Sources and How to Use Them* (4th edition) (Newton Abbott: David and Charles: 1989); D. N. Bradshaw *World Photographic Sources* (New York: Directories, 1984); J. Wall *Directory of British Photographic Collections* (London: Heinemann,1977); *The British Association of Picture Libraries and Agencies - List of Members, a Subject Index and Practical Guide to Libraries and their Users* (London: BAPLA, 1980) all of which include details of sports collections. At the local level, the *Merseyside Directory of Photographic Sources* provides a useful guide to collections on Merseyside, including the holdings of such sporting organisations as Everton and Liverpool football clubs. Local directories may exist for other areas.

Large general collections of photographs in Britain include: the photographic libraries of the Royal Photographic Society (The Octagon, Milton Street, Bath, BA1 1DN, Tel: 0225-62841); the Royal Commonwealth Society (currently being moved to University of Cambridge Library); the Royal Institute of British Architects and the Royal Town Planning Institute, (21 Portman Square, London W1, Tel: 071-580-5533); the Hulton Deutsch Collection (Unique House, 21-31 Woodfield Road, London W9 2BA, Tel: 071-266-2662), (sport in general) and the Mansell Collection (42 Linden Gardens, London W2 2ER, Tel: 071-229-5475) (sport in general particularly between 1900 and 1940). More specialised large collections include: for portrait photographs, the photographic library of the National Portrait Gallery (2 St Martin's Place, London, WC2H OHE, Tel: 071-230-1552); for aerial photographs, Aerophoto (Harrier House, 26 Blandy Avenue, Oxford, OX13 5BD, Tel: 0865-820729). Many national and local newspaper offices, as well as publishers of general and specialist sports periodicals (such as *Sports Illustrated, Canoeist,* etc.) maintain extensive photograph libraries, some of which are catalogued with helpful cross-referencing. The picture library of *The Daily Mail* is held in the John Rylands University Library, Manchester, where it is available for public consultation with prior permission. Unfortunately for the researcher, many private libraries insist on conducting requested searches themselves, inviting the customer to make a choice from a limited range easily identified. A charge is also usually made for this service. A small number of governing bodies of sport maintain photographic collections, although these vary in size and range. The BP Library of Motor Car Racing at Beaulieu has a large photographic collection.

Photographic collections within local libraries and record offices vary immensely. By far the largest and most comprehensive local record office collection in Britain is the Prints and Photograph section of the Greater London Record Office (40 Northampton Road, London, EC1R OHB, Tel: 071-633-3255). A valuable collection of family album photographs containing many sporting pictures mainly between the years 1880-1940 is housed at the Greater Manchester Record Office. M. W. Barley *A Guide to Britain Topographical Collection* (London, Council for British Architecture, 1974) lists collections of prints and photographs by counties.

In recent years a large number of albums illustrating the history of towns and villages have been published, which sometimes contain photographs revealing important detail of sporting events, personalities, venues, equipment and clothing. More specifically concerned with sport are N. Wigglesworth *Victorian and Edwardian Boating from Old Photographs* (London: Batsford, 1986) and J. N. P. Watson *Victorian and Edwardian Field Sports From Old Photographs* (London: Batsford, 1978). Many of these photographs are still in private hands and would not have otherwise been revealed to the researcher. A recent collection of photographs devoted entirely to sport in the Ancient World is R. L. Sturzebecker *Photo-Atlas of Athletic Cultural Archaeological Cities in the Greco-Roman World* (published by the author in 1985). This publication contains two thousand and ninety six black and white, and one hundred and sixty one colour photographs of sites of stadia, gymnasia, palestrae, circuses, hippodromes and the like, including some sites in Britain.

Films, Television and Videos

Sport has featured prominently in both film and television since the media was first invented. In 1987, according to the BBC Broadcast Research Department, 816 hours 37 minutes of BBC One air time were devoted to sport - that is 28.65 per cent of total BBC One broadcasting. Similar figures were produced for BBC Two - 34.22 per cent, I.T.V. 21.2 per cent and Channel Four - 16.01 per cent. (61) In addition to coverage of sporting events and the media's treatment thereof, researchers may be interested in consulting television documentaries about sport. Numerous such programmes have been produced, not all of which have been broadcast. Of those which have, the programme may include on a small fraction of the video footage shot for the programme. Although policies vary from one company to another, such footage is generally retained in the company's archive.

In terms of film collections, E. Oliver *Researcher's Guide to British Film and Television Collections* (4th edition) (London: British Universities Film and Video Council, 1989) is a useful starting place to locate suitable material. This guide is arranged according to the different types of archives. Each entry gives contacts, history, holdings, component details, cataloguing and access information. Also published by the British Universities Film and Video Council are J. Ballontye *Researcher's Guide to British Newsreels* (1983) and *Post-War British History: A Select List of Videos and Films Available in the UK* (in association with the Institute of Contemporary History, 1988). Bowker Saur produce an annual *Complete Video Directory* on CD-ROM. F. Thorpe *A Directory of British Film and Television Libraries* (Slade Film History Register, 1975) surveys the main existing sources of film and video, especially those useful for the study of history and sociology. The most extensive bibliography of sports videos is G. Blood (comp.), *Guide to Commercially Available Videotapes on Sport* (Canberra: Australian National Sports Information Centre, 1933). Although compiled and published in Australia, its coverage is worldwide and includes more videos from or on Britain than anywhere else. Large film collections in England include: the National Film Archive (81 Dean Street, London, WIV 6AA, Tel: 071-437-4355, part of the British Film Institute), the BBC Film and Video Tape Library (Reynard Mills Industrial Estate, Windmill Road, Brentford, Middlesex, TW8 9NF, Tel: 081-567-6655) and those of the many other major television companies. Granada Television Company, for example, produces printed catalogues of broadcasts. In the *World in Action* catalogue can be found a number of documentaries specifically about sport. A large and well indexed collection of films is the North West Film Archive at Manchester Metropolitan University. This collection contains many films exclusively devoted to, or depicting sporting activities and events in the north west during the 20th century. Details of individual films and videos are listed in the *British National Film and Video Catalogue* (London: British Film Institute, published annually since 1963). The Sports Council published a *Catalogue of Sports Films* (2nd edition) (London: The Sports Council, 1983) but unfortunately, this guide is not very comprehensive and contains little that will be of use to the sports historian. Unfortunately, considerable valuable film footage remains in private hands and is destroyed upon the death of the owner. Presumably this will become more common as the popularity of 'cam corders' becomes more popular. Finally, the North American Society of Sports Historians have for some years been compiling a bibliography of sports films which it is planned publish in 1994 (Metuchen, NJ; Scarecrow). Some film and television companies specialise in particular sports and maintain an extensive collection. 'Chrisfilms' of Pateley Bridge in Yorkshire, for example, have films and videos documenting most of the major championship events in white water canoeing over the past twenty five years.

A small number of governing bodies of sport have built up historical film collections, some of which are now in the process of being transferred to video tape, both for posterity and because a nostalgic commercial market has evolved. A fine example is the series marketed by the British Canoe Union. Some local libraries, record offices and museums collect film and video tapes on local events. The Llanelli Public Library, for example, has a collection of material on rugby in the region.

Although the value of film as a source of evidence has been recognised virtually since the medium was invented in the latter part of the 19th century, there are many dangers in the indiscriminate use of film, dangers not only apparent in the use of other source material without proper criticism, but dangers peculiar to the nature of the medium itself. Sports history researchers using film and other pictorial sources for the first time are therefore encouraged to seek guidance on their use and validity as a source of historical evidence. In addition to the more general guides to using historical sources (see p. 27) which often include sections on pictorial sources, researchers are advised to consult N. McCord "Photographs as Historical Evidence', *Local Historian*, 13, 1 (January 1978); G. Oliver *Photographs and the Local Historian* (London: Batsford, 1979); A. Elton "The Film as a Source Material for History' *Aslib Proceedings* VII (1955) pp. 207-239, P. Smith *The Historian and Film* (Cambridge University Press, 1976) and N. Poonay, B. R. Smith and T. Hastie *The Use of Film in History* (London: The Historical Association, 1972) to mention but a few.

Paintings and Prints
(Also see pp. 64-65)

As factual visual source material there is no distinction to be drawn between sporting paintings and sporting prints. Many of the prints were of course engraved after paintings, but while comparatively few paintings remain the prints, which were often published in thousands, have survived. Because of the cheapness and popularity of prints the number of commissions for designs grew to a positive flood, thus providing a great reservoir of visual information. Publishers like Orme, McLean and especially Rudolph Ackermann and Rudolph Ackermann Junior, commissioned a variety of sporting prints published in bound volumes or as single prints of high quality which are now collector's pieces. According to Ford, (62) sportsmen were for the most part literal and conservative in matters relating to their sports and their requirements for their representation were that they should have an accurate record rather than an imaginative treatment of the subject. Two of the most famous artists, Samuel Howitt and Henry Alken, produced hundreds of prints giving accurate portrayals, but they often managed to transcend this limitation and achieve imaginative and harmonious composition as well. Of great importance is the fact that the artists set the sports in their environments so that one can become aware of the relation of the physical environment to the sport, the social backgrounds of the participants. A fine example is the atmosphere of the Westminster cock-pit captured in Robert Cruikshank's work. At the racecourse the variety in the crowd can be noted in Pollard's series of racecourse prints: the carriages of the wealthy drawn up along the course, the stance of the blacklegs, the course attendants keeping back the crowd with their whips and a fist fight taking place between two of the mob while the horses race past. Finally, it is important to note the quite specific information about the techniques of sport which early prints and paintings provide. Thus in shooting prints and paintings before the end of the eighteenth century the sportsman holds his left hand near his right near the stock rather than further down the barrel, which had the unhappy tendency to split until the quality of steel began to improve by the end of the century. One notes the gradual reduction in the length of the barrel, the gradual appearance of the double barrel by the end of the eighteenth century, and much later the introduction of the breech loader in place of the muzzle loader with ram-rod and shot bag. Through paintings and prints one can trace the continuing breeding characteristics of the English thoroughbred racehorse, the hunter, the fox-hound and the gundogs. In cricket, the bowlers first bowl or roll the ball, then bowl round-arm. The shape of the bat then allied to the method of bowling the ball, explains the limitation on the shots that could be played and explains the low scores that were common to most games in the nineteenth century. The curiously stylised pose of the pugilist likewise explains the limitation in the movement of the prize fighters, whose battles were partly wrestling matches and involved little of the free movement of later boxing. The details of baiting sports, which would be particularly unfamiliar to us without the prints are brought to us in their fierce concentration and excitement by Alken and Charles Towne.

World Painting Index identifies details of and locations of famous paintings. Among the most notable collections of paintings and prints in Britain are the National Art Collection at the Victoria and Albert Museum, Cromwell Road, South Kensington, London, SW7 2RL, the British Museum and the National Portrait Gallery all of which include works on sport, boxing, cricket and horse racing being the best represented. All the collections are well indexed in terms of artist and subject matter. J. N. D. Watson

Collecting Sporting Art (London: Sportsman's Press, 1988) lists galleries with sporting collections and the British Sporting Art Trust, c/o The Tate Gallery, Mill Bank, London, SW7 2RL (Tel: 071-589-6371 ext. 262) maintains an inventory of sporting paintings in British galleries. In 1987, together with Boydell and Brewer, it published an *Inventory of Sporting Art in the Public Galleries in the UK* edited by G. Pendred. The most extensive collection of British sporting paintings is the one owned by the American millionaire Paul Mellon, details of which are included in J. Egerton *The Paul Mellon Collection, British Sporting and Animal Paintings, 1655-1867* (London: The Tate Gallery, 1978). Notable specialist collections of prints and paintings are at Lord's (cricket) and the National Horseracing Museum in Newmarket. Henderson and Stirk (63) provide short biographies of golf artists and an index to locations of pictures of golf and golfers prior to 1800. The United States of America has its own National Art Museum of Sport located in New York. A useful bibliography of American paintings is contained in H. L. Ray "Sport Art in the USA', *NASSH Proceedings*, (1983), pp. 18-19.

Paviere has compiled a *Dictionary of Sporting Painters* (Lewis, 1980). The American Library Association have produced a *Guide to the Literatue of Art History* (Chicago: ALA, 1980). *Art Index* (published since 1929 by H. W. Wilson) and *Art Literature Index* list secondary works on the history of art. *Art Index* is also now available on CD-ROM (via vendor Silver Platter).

Just as there are a large number of published photographic albums, so too are there a significant number of monographs illustrating famous and not so famous sporting paintings and prints. Examples include: D. Coombs *Sport and the Countryside in English Paintings, Watercolours and Prints* (Oxford: Phaidon, 1978), S. A. Walker *Sporting Art: England, 1700-1900* (London: Studio Vista, 1972), F. L. Wilder *English Sporting Prints* (London: Thames and Hudson, 1974) Auction and exhibition catalogues provide another useful source for the historian of sporting art. See for example the *Catalogue of Mr. and Mrs. J. R. Dick Collection of English Sporting and Conversation Paintings which will be Sold by Auction by Sotheby and Co., London; 1954;* P. Goldman *Sporting Life: An Anthology of British Sporting Prints* (London: Trustees of the British Museum, 1983) (based on an exhibition of sporting prints at the British Museum Department of Prints and Drawings in 1983), *British Sporting Painting, 1650-1850* (London: The Arts Council, 1974) based on an exhibition at the Hayward Gallery, London, 1974/75 and R. Simon and A. Smart *John Player Art of Cricket* (London: Secker and Warburg, 1983) based on an exhibition at the Fine Art Society Gallery (London) in 1983.

Advertisements (See p. 74)

Artefacts
(Also see Ephemera, Sports Costume, Sports Industry.)

'Artefacts' is a rather ambiguous term to use in the context of historical records since almost anything surviving from a bygone era may be included under this heading. In this instance, the term is used to refer specifically to three dimensional objects from the past. Items of clothing and equipment fall into this category. Such items, which often need to be examined in order to appreciate certain skills, patterns of play etc. are to be found in general and specialist, national and local, public and private collections.

Artefacts discovered by archaeologists have revealed extensive information about the practice of athletics in Ancient Greece. In the modern world several governing bodies of sport, individual clubs, manufacturers of sports equipment and stadia are beginning to take an interest in their heritage and are now building their own collections of historical material. The Memorial Gallery at Lord's is said to be the oldest museum of sport in Britain. It contains many artefacts including bats, balls and trophies from different periods, ties, badges, caps and other items of clothing, cigarette cards, bill posters, photographs and paintings, ceramic pieces, etc. Other sports museums exist at Newmarket (National Museum of Horse Racing, High Street, Newmarket, Tel: 0638-667333), Twickenham (Museum of Rugby Union, Whitton Road, Twickenham, TW2 7RQ, Tel: 081-892-8161), Huddersfield (Rugby League Hall of Fame), Rugby (Museum of Rugby Football), Wimbledon (The National Lawn Tennis Museum, Church Road, Wimbledon, London, SW19 5AE, Tel: 081-946-6131), Birmingham (National Centre for Athletics Literature, University Library, University of Birmingham, P. O. Box 313, Birmingham, B15 2TT, Tel: 021-472-1301 ext. 2205). Plans have recently been announced for a national museum of rowing to be established at Henley.

On a more local level, Liverpool and Manchester United football clubs, Old Trafford cricket ground and Wembley Stadium, York and Aintree racecourses have small historical collections of artefacts which may be consulted with prior approval.

Grays of Cambridge have their own private collection of racquets made by the company since its foundation and similarly, Pyrahana Mouldings of Runcorn have a historical collection of canoes (mainly their own models but also several owned by the Historic Canoe Association). Several such companies are usually prepared to allow the serious researcher to consult their collections by prior arrangement.

Unfortunately, the only way of finding out about these private collections is usually to write directly to the manufacturers themselves.

The Museum Association *Museum Yearbook* provides a useful directory of museums and galleries in the British Isles with a helpful subject index to special collections. Also included are details of addresses, opening hours and facilities.

In North America there are over two hundred Sports Museums and Halls of Fame devoted to individual sports (e.g. The Baseball Hall of Fame, Copperstown) sports within a particular state or town (e.g. The Texas Hall of Fame, Grand Prairie, The San Diego Hall of Champions) sport among a particular race, nationality (e.g. The National Polish American Sports Hall of Fame, Detroit, The International Jewish Sports Hall of Fame, Los Angeles) sport associated with a particular institution, venue or competition (e.g. USC Hall of Fame, Los Angeles, The Coliseum Hall of Fame, Los Angeles, The Rose Bowl Hall of Fame, Pasadena). G. Lewis and G. Redmond *Sporting Heritage - A Guide to Halls of Fame, Special Collections and Museums in the United States and Canada* (New Brunswick, NJ: A. S. Barnes, 1973), R. J. Higgs *Sport: A Reference Handbook* (Westport, CT: Greenwood Press, 1983) and P. Sodberg and H. Washington *The Big Book of Halls of Fame in the United States and Canada* (New York: R. R. Bowker, 1977) are helpful in identifying those collections likely to be of interest to the researcher. Since 1991, the *Journal of Sport History* has included a "Museum Reviews' section to explore the value of these collections to the sports historian.

In October 1989, a museum largely devoted to one particular sportsman, Sir Don Bradman was opened in Bowral, NSW, Australia.

Many items remain in private hands although these are sometimes on temporary loan to museums or touring exhibitions where they may be examined. Serious collectors often belong to organised groups to promote the collection and exchange of sports memorabilia. The Society of Olympic Collectors and the Cricket Memorabilia Society are two examples of organisations who might be prepared to help the serious researcher track down important items for examination. Finally, miscellaneous artefacts are described in collector's guides and in books about artefacts. Those of special interest to the sports historian include: B. R. Wynne *The Book of Sports Trophies* (London: Cornwall, 1984); *Billiards and Snooker, Cricket, Tennis, Squash* and *Badminton* in the *Shire Albums Series* (Princes Risborough) and such publications as B. R. Sugar *The Sport Collectors' Bible* (3rd edition) (Indianapolis: Bob Merrill, 1979); J. Taylor *Golf Collector's Price Guide* (Milton Keynes: St Giles Publications, 1983), L. T. Stanley *The Sporting Collector* (London: Pelham, 1984) and the recent *Wisden Guide to Cricket Memorabilia* (Oxford: Lennard, 1990).

A brief discussion of the value of sports museums and halls of fame to the historian of sport is discussed in: J. T. West "Halls of Fame in North America: Are They Relevant to the Sports Historian?', *NASSH Proceedings*, (1978), pp. 65-66. A number of other published articles describe the relevance of specific museums, collections within museums, collections relating to specific topics, (e.g. R. A. Howell "Women in Sport in the Ancient Western World in the British Museum', *Proceedings of the AAHPERD Congress*, New Orleans (1979) and W. J. Pesavento "The Field Museum of Natural History - Collections in Traditional Athletic Games of the Native American', *Proceedings of the AAHPERD Congress*, Kansas City (1978).

Ephemera

Ephemera are sometimes regarded as being of limited historical value. The term includes such items as match tickets, programmes and posters. J. Johnson whose magnificent collection of print ephemera on the printing industry was acquired by the Bodleian Library said of the term, 'It is difficult to describe except by saying that it is everything which would ordinarily go into the waste paper basket'. Throughout the world there are many serious collectors of items on specific sports and sporting events. Serious collectors in Britain often belong to the Ephemera Society, 12 Fitzroy Square, London, W1P 5HQ, Tel: 071-387-7723, which produces periodically a list of members with a subject index to their area(s) of interest. There is also a number of more specialist collector groups, in addition to the ones already mentioned in connection with artefacts, such as the Society of Olympic Collectors, the Cricket Memorabilia Society, the British Football Programme Collector's Club, the Rugby League Collector's Federation, etc.

Finally, it must not be forgotten that many sporting artefacts, photographs, along with other forms of manuscripts remain in private hands. Many sportsmen and women maintained scrapbooks of newscuttings, photographs, certificates, results sheets and other memorabilia associated with their sporting days. If the person has since died these have often been retained by relatives, some of whom with great pride may be only too happy to allow the serious researcher access to them. N. Parry's study of the 19th century Liverpool gymnast Alexander Alexander (64) drew considerable evidence from material contained in a trunk at the time in the hands of a niece. Harold Abrahams maintained his own archive which since his death has been deposited in with the National Centre for Athletics Literature at the University of Birmingham Library.

Maps, Plans and Drawings

In addition to photographs, paintings and prints; maps, plans and drawings may contain information of interest to the sports historian.

Several articles have been written which discuss the merits of using maps and plans for historical research. These include: J. B. Harley *Maps for the Local Historian: a Guide to British Sources*, and *The Historian's Guide to Ordnance Survey Maps* (The Standing Conference for Local History, 1972); D. Smith *Maps and Plans for the Local Historian and Collector* (London: Batsford, 1988); P. Hindle *Maps for the Local Historian* (London: Batsford, 1988) and a recent series on "Maps and Plans for Local History' by H. Nichols in the *Local History Magazine* (1990).

Before the 16th century there are virtually no regional maps, but many published since have included information of either direct or indirect value to the sports historian. Large scale ordenance survey maps of towns often included details of locations of bear pits, bowling alleys and cricket pitches. Maps and plans of estates often showed the extent of the stables, enclosures for hounds, terrain and habitats suited for supporting grouse, foxes, ducks, pheasants and other hunted creatures. From the 19th century maps were prepared to show locations of golf courses, horse-racing tracks, county cricket grounds. Sometimes these were published by rail companies to promote their services amongst sportsmen who were now travelling further afield to practise their sports or by breweries now organising sporting contests in order to increase their sales.

The library of the Royal Geographical Society has one of the largest general collections of maps in the UK, but probably the most useful one to the sports historian is the Maps Department of the British Library in Bloomsbury. Perhaps a major reason why maps and plans have not been extensively used by the sports historian is ignorance of their existence and the type of information they sometimes contain. This problem is undoubtedly exacerbated by the fact that they can be very difficult to trace from a subject point of view. First impressions of the library catalogue might suggest there is little of any value or that to locate those which are would be very time consuming. This is due to the fact that maps are usually catalogued topographically or by geographic name. Hence to find details of a map tracing the route taken by the 1953 expedition to the top of Mount Everest one is obliged to look under Everest, not mountaineering. Similarly, to discover maps prepared for canoeists or anglers, one is obliged to look under the name of each of the rivers concerned with the study.

Other sources of maps and plans in Britain, include the library of the Royal Town Planning Institute (26 Portland Place, London, W1N 4AE, Tel: 071-636-9107) and the many local record offices throughout the UK.

Patents

A patent protects the right of an individual to benefit from the usefulness of his invention by preventing exploitation of it by others, without permission, for a given period. It describes the invention and often contains diagrams and other illustrations. The value of patents in sports history research has been shown by I. T. Henderson and D. I. Stirk in their *Golf in the Making* (Crowley: Henderson and Stirk, 1979). Between 1844 and 1914, no fewer than seven hundred and eight patents were registered in the UK on just about every aspect of golf equipment. This included two hundred and twenty seven on golf balls, one hundred and seventy nine on golf clubs, fifty three on golf shafts, eighty on golf bags and one hundred and sixty nine on other miscellaneous items. However, it is important to stress that since the bulk of information is technical, patents are of little value for any other purpose. Historians interested in following up this line of enquiry are advised to consult F. Newby *How To Find Out About Patents* (Oxford: Pergamon, 1967) and the British Patents Office *About Patents as a Source of Technical Information* (London: HMSO, 1972). The British Library - Science Reference and Information Service Library has a large collection of patents with useful finding aids.

Legal Records

J. M. Carter in his *Ludi Medi Aevi; Studies in the History of Medieval Sport* (Manhattan, KS: MA/AH Publishing, 1981) has illustrated how Royal proclamations of many monarchs, the Liberate Rolls of King Henry III and the coroners' rolls are filled with insights into the Medieval sporting milieu. The coroners' rolls contain references to the various sports of the servile classes and the unfortunate deaths caused by them. The rolls of the justices in Eyre which date back to the twelfth century also contain vast amounts of detail about the sport and pastimes of peasant society.

Fortunately, many of these documents, stored in the Public Record Office, are available in print, either in full or in summary form. The Selden Society has published more than fifty volumes of judicial records of the thirteenth and fourteenth centuries, many county record societies have printed local selections from all types of early administrative documents and, above all, the Public Record Office has produced calendars of charters, etc from the twelfth or thirteenth to the sixteenth centuries. Calendars do not quote the full texts, but give the essential facts in each document.

Records of the major courts such as the county assizes are to be found in the Public Record Office (see p. 29), those of local courts such as the quarter sessions and magistrates court are usually held in the local record office. Although sporting venues were sometimes the scene of criminal acts and certain other sports were illegal practices in themselves (e.g. baiting sports in the later part of the nineteenth century) there is little to help the sports historian locate pertinent material without a previous lead to a particular individual. Legal records have, however enabled us to be well informed, perhaps even disproportionately, about those recreations which met with the disapproval of administrators, magistrates, priests and moralists, particularly during the Middle Ages.

Examples of other legal records relating to sport include licences and deeds of sports grounds, professional footballers' contacts and rights of access to footpaths, rivers and waterways for fishing, canoeing, etc. These can be found in solicitors' records deposited in local record offices.

Research Data

In 1937 a social science research organisation Mass Observation was set up to create what they called an 'anthology of ourselves'. One of the Mass Observation's interests was how people spent their leisure time and their studies therefore touch on sporting activities in many different ways throughout the 1938-1950 period. The papers generated by this work were deposited with the University of Sussex. Similarly, the Social Science Research Council set up a data archive at the University of Essex in 1967 to acquire, store and disseminate computer-readable copies of social science data sets for further analysis by the research community. This particular collection includes data from a project carried out at the University of Liverpool on the leisure patterns (including sport) of shift workers in Lancashire in the early 1980s. Such data may be of value to some sports historians. A useful publication in this respect is K. Schurer and S. J. Anderson *A Guide to Historical Data Files Held in Machine Readable Form* (Cambridge: Association for History and Computing, 1992)

Other Primary Sources

Finally, it is important to note that there are many other sources that can and have been put to good use in sports history research. Many such as census records have been extensively discussed in mainstream works on historical sources. The following articles illustrate just a few of the many other primary sources that historians of sport have found appropriate in their researches.

C. J. Gregory "Signs and Sporting Emblems', *Canadian Journal of the History of Sport and Physical Education*, VII, I (May, 1976), 22-32; H. Karl "Antique Greek Coins as a Source for the Historian', *Canadian Journal of the History of Sport and Physical Education*, X, 2 (December, 1987), 76-90; R. J. Shephard "Philately - A Possible Tactic for the Quantitative Study of Sports History', *Proceedings of the 5th Canadian Symposium on the History of Sport and Physical Education*, University of Toronto (August, 1982), pp. 237-448; D. B. Van Dalen "Political Cartoons Employing Sports as a Communications Media', *Canadian Journal of the History of Sport and Physical Education*, VII, 2 (December, 1976), 39-57.

Sports historians working in some areas, especially where source material appears to be totally lacking, have found it helpful to advertise in the press, especially, but not exclusively, the specialist press. Pritchard found this method most helpful in researching his history of croquet. (65)

Part IV - Sources for Specialist Areas of Research

This section is not intended comprehensively to discuss and list sources for all of the topics included, but simply to highlight the most pertinent sources and to identify reference works that provide the researcher with 'short-cuts' to appropriate information. It is intended to complement, rather than duplicate or offer an alternative to the earlier sections which discuss the nature of the source material itself.

Histories of Individual Sports

Sources of information for the history of individual sports vary immensely from activity to activity. Some sports have a rich and extensive literature of both primary and secondary sources. This includes information in the form of reference works, histories, manuscripts, often housed within special collections. Others have little obvious source material to draw upon (e.g. canoeing). Cricket is undoubtedly the most written about sporting activity in Britain, followed by association football, golf and horse racing. Field sports, including angling, also have an extensive literature.

A useful starting point for nation-wide histories of individual sports is often the library or archive of the governing body of the sport under investigation. Some governing bodies such as the Alpine Club, have extensive collections of both primary and secondary source material, others, such as the Amateur Swimming Association, have limited collections and some nothing at all. Not all governing bodies house their own collection. The Library of the Rock and Fell Climbing Club, for example, is held at the University of Lancaster Library and the manuscript records of the Table Tennis Association at the University of Liverpool Department of Archives. They may still be examined by members of the public who have been granted permission to consult them by the governing body. Those in public collections are listed in R. W. Cox (1993), updated in the *British Society of Sports History Bulletin* (now *The Sports Historian*) and many are included in the catalogues maintained by the NRA (see p. 27).

Tracing the history of individual sports at the recreational level is usually more difficult. Whilst professional clubs, as limited companies, are obliged by law to keep records for a minimum period of time, publish annual reports, etc. the same is not true of amateur clubs and leagues. A recent article on "Sources for the History of Recreational Cricket' by J. Williams published in the *British Society of Sports History Bulletin*, No. 8 (1988) describes some of the difficulties and suggests useful sources.

Field sports such as coursing, fox hunting, grouse shooting and animal sports such as bear-baiting, cock-fighting and ratting, which were important features of Britain's sporting heritage from the Middle Ages, were rarely centrally coordianted or controlled. Information on fishing rights, shoots, hunts, etc. is often contained in the private papers of prominent families who promoted such activities on their estates. Diaries, accounts, maps and plans, game books and correspondence with solicitors are all useful sources of information in this respect. Sources for the recreational activities of peasant and plebian classes are more difficult to find. Apart from newspapers which often reported on activities within the urban areas from the early part of the nineteenth century, one is restricted largely to the diaries, journals and sermons of church leaders and social reformers who sought to ban many such sporting activities. The Royal

Society for the Prevention of Cruelty to Animals was actively involved in bringing an end to many of the animal sports in the nineteenth century and published numerous pamphlets on the subject. R. W. Malcolmson provides a useful discussion on piecing information together on popular recreations, organised within an oral tradition (rather than an institutional framework), from scattered and fragmentary evidence in his *Popular Recreations in English Society 1700-1850* (Cambridge: Cambridge University Press, 1973, p. 3). Finally, it is perhaps also worth mentioning Peter and Iona Opie *Children's Games in Street and Playground* (Oxford: Clarendon Press, 1969) and Alice B. Gomme *The Traditional Games of England, Scotland and Ireland* (London: Thames and Hudson, 1984). These two publications may prove helpful to researchers exploring children's games and local traditions.

A number of points to be borne in mind in researching and writing histories of individual sports are discussed in an article by D. Voit. (66)

Histories of British Sport Overseas (Using British based sources) (67)
(Also see Manuscripts, Histories of Individual Tournaments, etc.)

The export of sport from Britain overseas via businessmen, missionaries, teachers and colonial administrators has been a topic of considerable interest in recent years. (68)

Historians interested in the history of sport in foreign nations are advised to search for similar sources identified for the history of sport in Britain. Although this should be possible for most industrialised nations it will be a problem for those researching the history of sport outside the developed world where sources are scarce and written documentation of events almost non-existent. In the absence of sources expressing alternative viewpoints, researchers should be wary of the problems of having to rely on the only sources that are available. As an example, historians interested in the development of sport and physical education in Ghana during British rule, have to rely almost entirely on 'British sources'. (69)

Basic background information relating to climate, education, the economy, population, etc. is contained in the *Statesman's Yearbook* , national encylopaedias (e.g. *Encyclopaedia Canadiana)* and official yearbooks produced by many individual countries. Mention has already been made of the fact that some national bibliographies (e.g. the *New Zealand National Bibliography*) list all material about as well as published in the country. Subject and source bibliographies, bibliographical series and national library catalogues similar to those discussed on previous pages in relation to Britain also exist for certain other countries (e.g. *Writings on American History*, (American Historical Association); J. H. St. J. McIlwaine *Theses on Africa, 1963-1975* (London: Mansell, 1978); *Africa Bibliography* (published annually by Manchester University Press on behalf of the International African Institute since volume 1984) and may be identified using some of the more general guides to literature listed on pp. 69-71. Clio Press *World Bibliographical Series* which intends to cover all countries of the world and has already published volumes for over one hundred different countries may be a useful starting point. Similar guides exist to primary material. A. L. P. Burdett *Summary Guide to Archive and Manuscript Collections Relevant to the Former British Colonial Territories in the UK* (London: Commonwealth Archivists Association, 1988) and more specifically, V. Bloomfields *Resources for Canadian Studies With Some Reference to Related Collections in Europe* (2nd edition) (London: British Association for Canadian Studies, 1983) are two such examples.

The value of resource centres in Britain, for the history of sport overseas vary immensely. The Libraries of the Royal Commonwealth Society (University of Cambridge Library) and the Commonwealth Institute, Kensington High Street, London, W8 6ND (Tel: 071-603-4535) contain useful background secondary literature on most countries of the British Commonwealth. The British Library has secondary literature on sport in many different countries, although in terms of foreign language material, the author is not in a position to pass informed judgement. The Official Publications Department of the British Library currently receives a comprehensive collection of publications from most governments of the world and the British Library Newspaper Library similarly receives the national daily newspapers of most nations. Some foreign embassies have libraries which allow consultation with prior permission although access policies do vary. Universities teaching area studies such as the University of London School of Oriental and African Studies usually have large library collections of secondary works which may prove useful. These and similar collections may be identified in the guides listed above. For researching the development of sport in the British Empire, valuable background material can sometimes be found in some of the Ministry libraries (the DFE Library, for example, has special reports on education overseas which includes a section on physical education in Ghana in the late nineteenth century), the library of the India Office, the library of the former Colonial Office, etc.

Many useful guides, indexes, publishing records, bibliographical series and national catalogues are to be found in British libraries. Examples of each type include P. Mander-Jones *Manuscripts in the British Isles Relating to Australia, New Zealand and the Pacific* (Canberra: 1972); Theses on the Commonwealth (London: University of London Institute for Commonwealth Studies, annually), *America: History and Life* (Santa Barbara, CA: Clio), *The Australian National Bibliography, Biblio-theque Nationale Catalogue General Des Livres Imprimes, 1897-1959* (and supplements).

A useful, although dated, bibliography of sports publications on different countries is: M. E. Herndon *Comparative Physical Education and International Sport* (Washington, DC: American Alliance for Health, Physical Education and Recreation, 1972). Maybe also of use is J. L. Arbena *An Annotated Bibliography of Latin American Sport: Pre-Conquest to the Present* (Westpoint, CT: Greenwood, 1989).

To assist with translations, F. Hepp *Sports Dictionary in Seven Languages* (English, German, Spanish, Italian, French, Hungarian and Russian) (London: Chambers, 1972) may be of some help.

Regional Histories of Sport
(Also see Local Government Records, History of Individual Sports, and Sport and Education)

The importance of local studies in the history of sport in Britain has been ably demonstrated by Bailey, (70) Meller (71) and Metcalfe. (72) Metcalfe's study of 19th century coal mining communities in Northumberland, for example, reveals that many of the nationally popular sporting activities failed to take a hold leaving traditional sporting pastimes such as cock-fighting and quoits to continue for some time after they had ceased to exist in the urban areas. P. and I. Opie and A. B. Gomme's books have already been mentioned as useful sources for background information on local traditions of sport, especially children's games (see p. 53).

A good starting place for a local history of sport is often the local studies collection at the local library. This may be housed at the local municipal or county library. In addition to collecting published works on local activities, events and personalities, they may contain copies of unpublished works such as theses, copies of small print run publications such as histories of local sports clubs, the transactions of local history groups, project work by local schools and adult education classes, collections of newspapers cuttings, none of which, as previously noted, find their way into indexes, bibliographies or major library collections.

Occasionally, the local studies librarian has had a personal interest in sport and has produced separate guides or reading lists of local material. Examples include the Guildford and Sheffield public libraries.

The local studies library or the local record office is also likely to house collections of local manuscripts that may be of some use to the sports historian. These may be records relating to individual clubs or the municipality as a whole. Many urban areas set up local sports councils and federations in the mid 1970s although some pre-date this decade by several years. The records of the Finchley Sports Federation, for example, date from 1935 and are to be found in the local history section of Barret Public Library. Again these can be identified in R.W. Cox *Sport: A Guide to Historical Sources in the UK* (1983) and updated in the *British Society of Sports History Bulletin* (-1992), and *The Sports Historian* (1993-), A very handy reference source for the local historian is S. Guy *English Local Studies Handbook. A Guide to Resources for each County including Libraries, Record Offices, Societies, Journals and Museums* (Exeter: University of Exeter Press, 1992).

The literature of some areas is much better documented than that of others. The Joint Committee on Lancashire Bibliography have published a series of bibliographies and guides to aid the local historian. Although none of their publications was specifically concerned with sport, they did include details of the records of local governments, businesses, etc., some of which had important sporting connections. Occasionally, university/polytechnic history departments teaching courses in local history have compiled bibliographies to assist students in their research. By way of example, in 1980, the Department of Economics and Economic History at Manchester Polytechnic compiled a *Checklist of Theses on the History of Lancashire* which contains useful references to sport. The Manchester Metropolitan University library, as it is now known, also maintains an extensive collection of local material with valuable guides to information on specific topics.

Other examples include E.H. Cordeaux and D.H. Merry *Bibliography of Printed Works Relating to the City of Oxford* (Oxford: Clarendon Press 1976). One or two such as E. Darroch and B. Taylor *Bibliography of Norfolk History* (Norwich: Centre for East Anglian Studies, University of East Anglia) plan to be ongoing, publishing supplements on a regular basis or from time to time. The Bibliography of Printed Works on London History project currently being undertaken by the Centre for Metropolitan History (34 Tavistock Square, London, WC1H 9EZ, Tel: 071-636-0272) maintains an online index to secondary literature on the history of London which includes many references to sport. Plans are afoot to publish a hard bound volume in 1994.

As noted above, several regional bibliographies have also been prepared as theses for Fellowships of the Library Association. Several, such as the ones for Blackpool, Wigan and Orpington in Kent contain numerous references to sport. FLA theses are held in the Library of the Library Association at

7 Ridgmount Street, London, WC1E 7AE. Researchers are advised to consult the index to FLA theses compiled by P.J. Taylor (see p. 12). More recent theses can be identified in the Library Association Library catalogue.

Many secondary sources may be identified using A. L. Humphreys *Handbook of County Bibliography: Being a Bibliography of Bibliographies Relating to the Counties and Towns of Great Britain and Ireland* (London, 1917), its successor G.H. Martin and S. McIntyre *Bibliography of British and Irish Municipal History* (Leicester: Leicester University Press, 1972) and the two updated by consulting the bibliography of "Recent Publications in Local History' published in *Local Historian*; the "Bibliography of Urban History' published annually in *Urban History Yearbook*; the Royal Historical Society *Writings on British History* and the *Annual Bibliography of British and Irish History* (see p. 9). *The County Magazine Index* (London: Clover Publications, 1979-) provides an index to magazines covering the rural and country life of the counties of England. It indexes approximately thirty magazines and lists in the region of three thousand, five hundred articles a year. Although essentially journalists articles, it does often include material on sport and can trigger off useful topics and avenues to explore.

A number of short monographs and articles on sports history have been published by local history societies in recent years. Those published before 31/12/1988 are listed in R.W. Cox (1991) they may be updated using bibliographical series appearing in *Northern History, The London Journal, Midland History, Southern History, Manchester Region History Review*, etc. (see p. 11). A certain amount of ongoing research, usually funded academic projects, is reported in "Current Research' in *Local History News*. More general items can be identified in E. L. G. Mulling *Guide to Historical and Archaelogical Publications of Societies in England and Wales* (London: Athlone Press, 1968) and updated in the sources listed above. A directory of local societies is provided by M. Pinhorn *Historical, Archaeological and Kindred Societies: A List* (Hulverstone Manor, Isle of Wight: Pinhorn, 1986).

General guides to primary sources for the local historian include: S. Guy *English Local Studies Handbook: An Essential Guide for Information for Professional and Amateur Local Historians* (Exeter: University of Exeter Press, 1992), W. B. Stephens *Sources for English Local History* (2nd edition) (Cambridge: Cambridge University Press, 1981); J. Richardson *The Local Historian's Encyclopaedia* (New Barnet: Historical Publications Limited, 1986) and numerous articles published in *Local Historian*. Although none of these publications specifically discusses sport, they do provide useful guides to background information on education, industry, the economy, etc. More specialised regional guides include such publications as K. Leslie and T. J. McCann *Local History in West Sussex: A Guide to Sources* (2nd edition) (Chichester: West Sussex County Council, 1985); D. J. Clayton "Sources for the History of the North West in the John Rylands University Library of Manchester', *Bulletin of the John Rylands University Library Manchester*, 71, 2 (Summer, 1989), 181-203 and J. S. Moore *Avon Local History Handbook* (London: Phillimore, 1979), the last having a small section on Leisure and Recreation (pp. 91-95) compiled by J.H. Bettey.

The *Volumes of the Victoria History of the Counties of England*, published since the turn of the century, often provide useful starting points for the local historian of sport. Volumes containing sections on the History of Sport and Pastimes are included in R. W. Cox (1991) and discussed in an article by the author entitled "Victoria County Histories as a Starting Point for the Local Historian of Sport', in the *British Society of Sports History Bulletin*, 2, (July, 1984). In 1989, the VCH celebrated the publication of its 200th volume. For each of the counties covered there is published, or planned, a set of volumes which includes both general articles treating topics like Domesday for the county as a whole, and topographical articles systematically covering every place in the county, parish by parish. The histories of parishes and towns are the speciality of the VCH. For the places they cover they provide a reliable outline of essential facts about the history of particular places and a quarry of references which act as indispensable starting points for further research.

Many local record offices have published guides to and catalogues of their individual collections which may help the researcher. One example is the Chester Record Office (see: A. M. Kennets *Archives and Records of the City of Chester* (Chester: Chester Record Office, 1985). The most comprehensive collection of such guides, outside the National Register of Archives (see pp. 27-28) is at the University of London Institute of Historical Research Additionally, local history groups sometimes publish guides and bibliographies of materials on selected topics and to special collections contained within the local record office. Many such guides, together with news of recent acquisitions, megers, etc. is contained in *The Local Studies Historian* (1982-). An index to the first ten volumes (1982-91) was published in 1992. The range and value of manuscript sources for the local history of sport contained within the records of the county record office are illustrated in an article entitled "Sport in Surrey' by D. A. Robinson which appeared in *The British Society of Sports History Bulletin*, No. 3 (January, 1985), 1-35. A useful guide to local newspapers and periodicals, additional to the more general guides listed above, is D. Dixon *Local Newspapers and Periodicals of the 19th Century: A Checklist of Holdings in Provincial Libraries* (University of Leicester Victorian Studies Centre Handlist No. 6) (Leicester: University of Leicester, 1973).

Histories of Sport in Individual Religions, Races, Tribes and Other Special Communities and Institutions
(Also see Sport and the Armed Services, Sport and Education, Sport and Industry)

Whilst the history of sport in individual religions, races, tribes and other special communities has proved a popular and fruitful avenue for reserach in Australia, Canada and the United States, (73) relatively little substantial work has so far been undertaken into the history of sport in particular religious, racial or other such groups in Britain.

A general reference work to assist the researcher studying religion and sport is C. J. Adams *Reader's Guide to the Great Religions* (2nd edition) (London: Collier Macmillan, 1977). Current awareness publications include P. Grimwood-Jones *Arab Islamic Bibliography* (Hassocks: Harvester, 1977) and the "Mormon Bibliography', published in *Brigham Young University Studies*. Reference works specifically related to sport in minority groups overseas are: *The Encyclopaedia of Jews in Sport*; L. G. Davis and S. Daniels *Black Athletes in the United States - A Bibliography of Books, Articles, Autobiography and Biographies on Black Professional Athletes in the United States 1800-1981* (Westport, CT: Greenwood Press, 1981) and A. Gilmore *The Afro-American in Sport: An Annotated Bibliography* (New York: Garland, 1986). More general guides containing references to sport include: A. Miller *Comprehensive Bibliography for the Study of American Minorities* (New York: University Press, 1976) and C. R. H. Taylor *A Bibliography of Publications on the New Zealand Maori* (Oxford:

Clarendon, 1972). A group totally overlooked to my knowledge, but undoubtedly worthy of investigation are gypsies. A useful starting point in this respect might be D. Kennington *Gypsies and Travelling People* (3rd edition) (London: Capital Planning Information, 1986) which provides a guide to documentary and organisational sources of information. There are several bibliographies on immigrants and minorities in Britain such as R. Madon *Coloured Minorities in Britain: A Comprehensive Bibliography, 1970-1977* (London: Aldwych Press, 1979) and V. F. Gilbert and D. Singh *Immigrants, Minorities and Race Relations: A Bibliography of Theses and Dissertations Presented at British and Irish Universities, 1900-1981* (London: Mansell, 1984). Unfortunately, neither mention sport but provide a useful guide to literature on the social and cultural background to some of these groups.

Manuscript material relating to sport and religion, on the whole, is restricted to the Anglican Church's condemnation of various sporting activities. The Methodist Archive in the John Rylands University Library, Manchester, for example, contain documents that bear witness to attempts by prominent Methodists to outlaw the practise of various blood sports. A limited amount of material, largely minutes of church sports clubs, is held at the Friends House in Euston Road, London, NW1 2BJ, Tel: 071-387-3601.

Many large organisations and employers such as the armed services, schools, hospitals, universities, manufacturing companies, the fire brigade and the police force have made provision for sport. Many youth groups such as the Boy's Brigade and Scouting movement organised sporting activities on a local, regional and national basis. Professional associations and chambers of commerce have also been known to organise competitions and tournaments for their members. Where this has been the case, files containing records of one form or another on sport are to be found in the company/institutional archives. The records of the Metropolitan Police Force, for example, contain considerable detailed information on different aspects of sporting activity with the force (e.g. MEOP 3730-3797). A useful guide in this respect is I. Brideman and C. Emsley *A Guide to the archives of the Police Forces of England and Wales* (Police History Society, 1989). In addition to R. W. Cox (1993), a useful guide to university records is A. R. Allan *University Bodies - A Survey of Inter and Supra University Bodies and their Records* (Liverpool: University of Liverpool Archives Unit, 1990). Archives of many large manufacturing businesses are listed in L. Richmond and B. Stockford *Company Archive* (see p. 74). The Scouting Movement has an extensive archive at their headquarters (Baden Powell House, Cromwell Road, South Kensington) and the records of such organisations as the Liverpool Law Golfing Society or the Merseyside Youth Association are deposited in the local record office. For the history of sport in the armed services see p. 66, for the history of sport in schools see Sport and Education (pp. 68-71).

Histories of Individual Sports Clubs, Teams and Other Institutions

Sources for the history of individual clubs and teams depends upon the nature and extent of the records that have been kept and preserved by that organisation. Many small local sports clubs run by volunteers, often without a ground or clubhouse of their own, did not bother to keep records. Indeed, it was not until the Victorian era that clubs organised themselves along democratic principles with committees producing records such as minutes and accounts. Furthermore, their activities did not demand formal record. If they did, these have sometimes been lost, destroyed or withheld as confidential. The MCC is a major exception to much of what has already been said. Although it lost its early records in a fire in 1816, it has maintained an extensive archive which is catalogued (soon to be available on-line) and is professionally staffed. Several of the county cricket clubs also have extensive and well managed archives. A small number of sports clubs had the foresight to deposit their records with the local record office where they have been sorted and in most instances catalogued. This is particularly the case in Scotland where the National Register of Archives (Scotland) approached many of the governing bodies of sport and local clubs with a view to sorting their records for them. It must be remembered, however, that as previously noted, many sports clubs are suspicious of outside inquirers and may refuse, as is their prerogative, to give access to their records to even the most prominent and well intentioned historian. If they are a registered company (limited or unlimited), as is the case with professional clubs, then statutory records including details of capital, names and addresses of shareholders and directors, annual accounts, auditors reports, etc, will be deposited with Companies House (Crown Way, Maindy, Cardiff, CF4 3UZ, Tel: 0222-388588) and may be consulted by any bona fide researcher. The files of defunct companies are kept by the Register of Companies until they are about twenty years old and then transferred to the Public Record Office. The files of dissolved companies are located in PRO classes BT31 and BT41 (see p. 29). (See the section on the history of sports industry pp. 73-74).

Where they do exist, club records often contain little more than committee minutes and, as pointed out by Wigglesworth (74) provide variable reading with some being full of much procedural waffle and some of unnecessary notes of an annoying nature. (75) Occasionally one may come across sets of club rules, fixture lists, posters, programmes, honours lists, scorebooks, certificates, membership lists, articles of association, ledgers and even cuttings books. Photographs, particularly of teams, are sometimes included but usually without any supporting information. In fact, the local newspaper is usually far more informative about the activities of local clubs in this sense. The nature and management of club records in the UK is discussed at greater length in R. W. Cox "A Model for Sports History Documentation', *International Journal of the History of Sport* 9, 2 (August, 1992), 252-279.

Meckler have recently published two encyclopaedias of major league baseball team histories edited by Peter Bjarkman (one devoted to the American League, one to the National League) and two bibliographies devoted solely to material on the history of two particular sports clubs. They are J. R. Schmidt *White Sox Bibliography* (1989) and M. Smith *The Dodgers Bibliography* (1989).

Histories of Individual Tournaments, Competitions and Venues

The Olympic and Commonwealth Games
Although international, the Olympic Games are included here because they are by far the most written about sport competition in the world. Many sports historians have shown interest in Britain's involvement in one capacity or another (76) and as a popular area of research, it was felt that no guide to sources would be complete without mention of them.

Numerous reference sources exist which should enable the researcher to get his hands on some significant information rapidly. E. S. Meyer "The Olympic Games: A Select Bibliography of Bibliographies', *Reference Services Review*, (Summer, 1984), pp. 95-99 and B. Mallon *The Olympics: A Bibliography* (New York; Garland, 1984) which list publications on the Olympic Games, including the publications of most national Olympic associations and the official reports of the organising committees who have been responsible for staging the Games, provide useful starting points. *Olympic*

Review, published quarterly by the International Olympic Committee, frequently includes short articles of a historical nature and details of memorabilia.

Other reference sources of possible interest include: W. J. Carroll *The Olympic Film Finder* (New York: Olympic Media Information, 1981); D. Wallechinsky *The Complete Book of the Olympic Games* (New York: Viking, 1984), *The Encyclopaedia of the Olympics*; N. D. McWhirter *Guinness Book of Olympic Records* (Enfield: Guinness Superlatives, published every four years) and J. Benagh *Incredible Olympic Feats* (New York: McGraw Hill, 1976). D. Matz *Greek and Roman Sport: A Dictionary of Athletes and Events form the Eighth Century BC to the Third Century AD* (Jefferson, NC: MacFarland, 1991) lists winners of the stade race at each of the Olympic festivals.

In terms of primary sources, the International Olympic Committee have a large archive at their Lausanne Headquarters (Chateau de Vidy), most national Olympic Associations maintain their own archives (the British Olympic Association archive is at 1 Church Row, Wandsworth Plane, London, SW18 1EH) and for every 'Games' Official Reports are produced by the Organising Committee. An important collection of manuscripts is the Avery Brundage collection, containing files on all aspects of the Olympic Games, including details of delicate negotiations through some very turbulent and difficult times, housed at the University of Illinois, Champaign. (77) R. L. Morrison compiled a useful, but highly specialised bibliography of *Government Documents Relating to the 1980 Olympic Games Boycott* (Washington DC: US Government Printing Office, 1983). Documents relating to Britain's involvement with the Olympic Games movement are to be found in the records of the Home Office (regarding public order at the 1908 and 1948 Olympic Games) and the records of the Foreign Office (regarding diplomatic issues) (see pp. 38-39).

There is a museum dedicated to the modern Olympic movement and an International Olympic Academy (IOA) with its own library both situated in Olympia, Greece. The IOA hosts an annual congress in Olympia which is attended by delegates from around the world presenting papers on all aspects of the Olympic movement, including historical analyses. A number of individual countries stage their own Olympic Academies, the first one in Britain taking place in Cardiff in 1983. The Proceedings of the IOA are published and those of some of the national academies. Several museums of sport and special collections dealing with individual sports also contain information relating to the Olympic Games and other major competitions in respect of their own individual concerns. A Society of Olympic Collectors exists to collect and exchange memorabilia.

In 1992 *Olympika: The International Journal of Olympic Studies* was launched by the Centre for Olympic Studies at the University of Western Ontario and in June 1993, a new multi-million pound Olympic movement was opened in Laussanne.

The records of the Commonwealth (formerly British Empire) Games which have been staged on British soil on several occasions (Cardiff 1958, Edinburgh 1970 and 1986) are housed at the headquarters of the Commonwealth Games Federation which shares the same address as the British Olympic Association (see above).

Other Competitions
Although the Medieval tournament started as a wild, tough brawl, it grew in time into a great spectator

sport with strict rules enforced by officials. Books, diaries, judicial records, verse and prose have all been successfully used to piece together information on the Medieval tournament.

Histories of other relatively recent, although more domestic sporting festivals, such as the Robert Dovers Games, the Scottish Highland Games and the Liverpool Olympic Games have been able to draw upon a wide range of primary source material such as family and estate papers, minute books, programmes and newspaper articles.

Short histories of a number of local sporting venues are included in the directories mentioned on p. 6.

Venues

In terms of primary sources, whilst the sites of the Pan Hellenic festivals have been extensively excavated and remnants put on display at the sites and in museums, little research has been undertaken about other sporting venues. Researchers may find useful source material in local record offices and for better known stadiums, in the library of the Royal Institute of British Architects (see p. 66). This library contains drawings and photographs of several sports buildings, including such famous landmarks as the White City and Crystal Palace. Unfortunately, for most sports historians, these collections are catalogued by the name of the architect, although a certain amount of subject indexing has been carried out. The records of the many dog and horse racing courses that once or even still exist in the UK are to be found in the archive of the companies that run or once ran them, an example being the Manchester Racecourse Company. Many of these have been deposited in the local record office. Less well established venues such as the many bowling alleys, cock-pits, etc. that once existed are sometimes to be found on local maps, plans and drawings (see p. 49), or mentioned in local directories (see p. 36), the papers of solicitors, landowners, etc. when leases were granted (see p. 29).

Mention has already been made of the increasing number of museums dedicated to particular teams and venues within the section on artefacts (see pp. 46-48). Several of these also contain manuscript material specifically relating to the history of the competition staged at the venue or the venue itself. A small collection of items relating to the Much Wenlock Olympics is held in the Much Wenlock Museum (High Street, Much Wenlock, Shropshire, Tel: 0952-727773).

Biographical Studies

Biographical studies of famous athletes, trainers, coaches, officials, adminstrators, punters, journalists, famous dogs and horses in respect of their sporting careers have proved popular topics of research during recent years. Thurmond's study of North American sports history (see p. 21), found it to be the most popular area of research. Unfortunately, few biographical works have explored the lives of famous sportsmen and women in relation to their times. Guttmann has described most sports biographies as "exercises in hagiography or public relations rather than scholarly assessments'. Similarly, Park has described studies of physical educationalists as largely "self-congratulatory paens to early leaders'. The fact is that most biographical studies, like most histories, are written for the popular and commerical market. Commenting on the American scene, Guttmann believes that several of the best sports biographies have been written by alienated players angry about the treatment they received. The same is true of works published in Britain. Certainly, Jim Guthrie *Soccer Rebel* (London: Pentagon, 1976), and Jimmy Hill *Striking for Soccer* (London: Sportsman's Book Club, 1963) provide more insight into professional soccer, and one more thought-provoking than say Bobby Charlton *Forward for England* (London: Pelham, 1967). Perhaps it is important to appreciate that at the time many famous sportsmen and women choose, or are encouraged to write their biographies (usually when approaching or shortly after reaching their peak), they are still very young, some in their early twenties, with limited experience of life in general and without the enquiring, analytical mind that is usually associated with age and experience.

In order to identify useful sources of biographical information the following publications are particularly helpful: R. B. Slocum *Biographical Dictionaries and Related Works: An International Bibliography of Collective Biographies, Bio Bibliographies, Collections of Epitaphs, Selected Genealogical Works, Biographical Indexes and Selected Portrait Catalogues* (2nd edition) (Detroit, MI: Gale Research, 1986) and D. J. Cimbala *Biographical Sources: A Guide to Dictionaries and Reference Works* (Phoenix, AZ: Oryx Press, 1988). (78)

Brief details of many famous individuals can be traced in biographical dictionaries and in encylopaedias. Literally thousands exist worldwide. Dictionaries of national biography are a useful quick reference source of information although it must be stressed that few sportsmen and women find their way into these reference works. (79) D. Banks of the University of Glasgow is currently in the process of compiling an occupational index to the *Dictionary of National Biography* (to be published by Oxford University Press) which includes sport as a separate category. Similar reference works exist for other countries such as *The Dictionary of American Biography, The Australian Dictionary of National Biography, The Dictionary of South African Biography*, etc. Similarly, there are a large number of *Who's Who* and *Who Was Who* series. These include the *Who's Who in History* series with separate volumes covering the periods: 55BC-1485, 1485-1603, 1603-1714, 1714-1789, 1789-1837, (Oxford: Blackwells) and the *Who Was Who* series with volumes for: 1897-1916, 1916-1928, 1929-1940, 1941-1950, 1951-1960, 1961-1970, 1971-1980. These are usefully indexed in *Who Was Who: A Cumulated Index 1897-1980* (1981). It is perhaps worth noting that not all who appear in *Who's Who* found their way into *Who Was Who* after their death. (80) Once again there are few individuals included because of their sporting prowess, but several who state sport as one of their chief interests. Other general biographical dictionaries including details of sporting personalities include: H. Oxbury *Great Britons* (Oxford: Oxford University Press, 1985) and A. Crawford *Biographical Dictionary of British Women* (London: Europa Publications, 1983). It may be that the researcher requires to check whether an individual belonged to a particular category or group of people in which case there are also more specialist biographical dictionaries relating to wealth, religion, political leanings. (81)

In addition to the international and national biographical dictionaries are many local directories and dictionaries based on regions or individual institutions which provide brief biographical details. Examples of local biographical dictionaries include: *Yorkshire Leaders, Yorkshire Men of Mark*, etc. (82)

The British Biographical Archive Series (London: Bowker Saur) provides on microfische details of 150,000 biographies compiled from hundreds of sources published between 1601 and 1978. The great majority of these lives fall within the period 1870 to 1960. *The British Biography Index* (London: Bowker Saur, 1991) compiled by L. Baille provides a quick reference source to archives. Similar series have been compiled for many other countries and are also published by Bowler-Saur. Publications dealing specifically with sport (and in addition to the encylopaedias and dictionaries of sport listed earlier which often include biographical summaries of famous individuals) are: listed in R. W. Cox *Sport in Britain* (1991), S. F. Wise and D. Fisher *Canada's Sporting Heroes* (Don Mills, Ontario, General Publishing Company for Canada's Sporting Hall of Fame) and R. Hickok *Who Was Who in American Sport* (New York: Hawthorne Books, 1971).

More specialist reference works based on particular sports, roles within those sports, nationality, place of birth, club, team or other features, or a combination of more than one of these characteristics also exist, although these contain varying amounts of detail. (83) The Association of Cricket Statisticians and Historians have published a series of county cricketers (e.g. M. G. Lorimer *Lancashire Cricketers, 1865-1988)* and documenting famous cricketer's records, e.g. *Innings by Innings* (e.g. A Hignell *J. C. Clay: His Record Innings by Innings* , 1991).

A recent series entitled *The Biographical Dictionary of American Sports* has been launched by Greenwood Press. Each volume contains several hundred biographical essays, including a systematic sketch of each subject's career and a brief bibliography. So far, volumes have appeared for baseball, football, outdoor sports and indoor sports (Westport, CT: Greenwood Press).

Obituaries are another source of select biographical information. Obituaries from *The Times* may be identified in F. Roberts (ed.) *Obituaries From The Times, 1951-60* (London: Newspaper Archive Developments Ltd) and its supplements (1961-1970, 1971-1975). The first two volumes feature about one thousand, five hundred obituaries in each and the last approximately one thousand. Some 60% of these are of eminent British subjects including some sportsmen and women.

Obituaries of ninety two famous American sports 'heroes' are reproduced in K. Arleen and J. Cohen *The New York Times Sports Hall of Fame* (New York: Arna Press, 1981). A selection of obituaries of cricketers appearing in *Wisden Cricketers' Almanack* are reprinted in B. Green (ed.) *The Wisden Book of Cricketers' Lives* (London: Queen Anne, 1988). Deaths omitted from the *Wisden Cricketers' Almanack* are listed in a series by that title in *The Cricket Statistician*. The scope and reliability of obituaries as well as entries in dictionaries of national biography varies immensely and should be carefully appraised in most instances.

Select bibliographies of secondary works which include biographical studies of sportsmen and women are: *Biographical Books, 1950-1980* (London: R. R. Bowker, 1980) (which includes name, author, title and vocation indexes); the British Library *Bibliography of Biography 1970-1984* (London: British Library, 1985 and annual supplements) (a computer generated microfiche bibliography of biographical works appearing in the *British National Bibliography* since its inception in 1951) (This product is also now available on CD-ROM via Chadwyck-Healey); J. Burnett, *Useful Toil: Autobiographies of Working People from the 1820s to the 1920s*, London (1974); J. Burnett, et al, *The Autobiography of the Working Class: An Annotated Critical Bibliography* three vols (1750-1900, 1900-1945, Suppl. 1750-1945) (1984, 1987, 1989); M. Hackett, *Nineteenth Century British Working Class Autobiographies: An Annotated Bibliography* (New York: AMS Studio in Social History, 1985); W. Matthews *British Autobiographies: An Annotated Bibliography of British Autobiographies Published or Written Before 1951* (Berkeley, CA: University of California Press, 1955). Other works include: J. V. Reel

Index to Biographies of Englishmen 1000-1485 found in Dissertations and Theses (Westport, CT: Greenwood, 1975); B. Nagle *The Gentleman's Magazine - Biography and Obituary Notices 1781-1819* (New York: Garland, 1981), R. Baker *Biographies of Historical Leaders in Health, Physical Education and Recreation*, Ed.D. thesis, Brigham Young University, 1971 and M. Trekell "A Representative Sampling of Biographical Theses and Related Articles, Books, Microfilms in Physical Education and Sport' in E. F. Zeigler *Research in the History, Philosophy and International Aspects of Physical Education and Sport: Bibliographies and Techniques* (Champaign, IL: Stipes Pub. Co., 1971). Details of biographical studies of famous sports women are included in M. Remley *Women in Sport* (Detroit, MI: Gale Research Co., 1980) and M. Shoebridge *Women and Sport: A Select Bibliography* (London: Mansell, 1987). Very famous sportsmen and women have occasionally had bibliographies compiled of their works or works about them. A fine example is L. G. Davis *Joe Louis: A Bibliography of Articles, Books, Pamphlets, Records and Archival Materials* (Westport, CT: Greenwood Press, 1983). Greenwood Press publish a series entitled *Popular Culture Bio Bibliographies* which contain valuable bibliographical essays. Several sportsmen have appeared in the series although so far these have been restricted to famous American nationals. (84) The only bibliography specific to a British national known to the author is J. H. St. J. McIlwaine serial "Bibliography of Neville Cardus', published in *The Cricket Quarterly*. (1964/65).

All known substantial biographical studies (including biographical dictionaries and collective studies but not obituaries and individual entries from biographical dictionaries) memoirs, published diaries, etc. of British born sportsmen and women appearing in print before 31/12/1988 are listed in R. W. Cox *Sport in Britain* (1991) and updated in the *British Society of Sports History Bulletin* (1989-92) and *The Sports Historian* (1993-). This does not, however, include short articles appearing in popular association football and cricket magazines. Researchers interested in identifying articles appearing in the biographical series listed on p. 19 are advised to consult the indexes to these magazines mentioned on the same page.

For updating existing bibliographies and identifying recently published material, *Biography Index* (published quarterly with annual cumulative volumes by H. W. Wilson since 1946) is an invaluable reference source. This bibliographical service indexes over two thousand, six hundred periodicals and newspapers. It includes collective and individual biographies, diaries and letters and is international in scope, although undeniably has a rather strong North American bias. This product is also now available on CD-ROM (via Silver Platter).

A. Guttmann in his study of Avery Brundage (*The Games Must Go On: Avery Brundage and the Olympic Movement* New York: Columbia University Press, 1984) makes extensive use of the private papers deposited by the former President of the International Olympic Committee, in the library of the University of Illinois at Champaign (see M. Brichford *Avery Brundage Collection* (1977) ibid. and p. 60). Unfortunately, few other sportsmen, or sportswomen after their death have left behind extensive archive material. Few of the small number who did, have deposited their papers in record offices.

For specifically identifying primary sources, the following guides exist although it must be stressed that few, if any, contain material specific to individual sportsmen and/or women. They are included here because some biographers are also interested in the sporting lives of individuals who were not renowned primarily for their sporting prowess but who commented on the subject or for whom it played an important part in their lives. Examples include: P. Hepworth *Select Biographical Sources* (London: Library Association, 1971) (This publication lists the whereabouts of the private papers of many well known leaders in British Society), W. Matthews *British Diaries: An Annotated Bibliography of British Diaries Written Between 1442 and 1942* (Berkeley, CA: University of California Press, 1950) and J. S. Batts *British Manuscript Diaries of the 19th Century* (1976). The National Register of Archives maintains a computerized personal names index relating to the location of personal papers and the papers of several prominent statesmen have been microfilmed by Harvester Press.

Mention has already been made of oral history techniques in generating historical evidence (see pp. 40-41) and this is a technique that has particular value in biographical research of living individuals. (85) Pictorial evidence of famous individuals including sportsmen and women exists at the National Portrait Gallery in London (86) as well as in some local record offices and archives of governing bodies of sport. Similarly, oral recordings and cine film or video recordings may sometimes be found in the archives of the British Institute of Recorded Sound, The British Film Institute, local record offices and the governing bodies of sport.

Part V - Brief Notes on Sources of Information for Specific Topics of Sports Historical Research

This section attempts to provide only very brief notes on sources for more specialised topics of historical research. Obviously, there are an infinite number of topics one could include; here is just a selection.

Sports Architecture

The history of architecture is amongst the best documented areas of research. Unfortunately, apart from M. Wymmer *History of Olympic Buildings* (Edition Leipzig, 1976), and the directories of sports grounds mentioned on p. 6 it is a much neglected line of investigation in sports historical research. Perhaps in the aftermath of the Hillsborough disaster in which ninety six football fans were killed in April 1989, new research will be stimulated to help further our understanding of why sports grounds and stadiums were designed, built and managed as they were. Almost certainly their size, geographical location and layout were determined by important social and economic considerations. It would also possibly help our understanding of what effect if any segregated seating had on the attitudes and behaviours of spectators at sporting events. Mention has already been made of the important collections of books, plans, drawings and photographs held by the Royal Institute of British Architects (see p. 49) which are also described in A. Mase *The RIBA: A Guide to its Archives and History* (London: Mansell, 1986). Valuable reference sources include: R. H. Kamen *British and Irish Architectural History: A Bibliography and Guide to Sources of Information* (1981), L. Woodhouse *British Architects, 1840-1976: A Guide to Information Sources* (Detroit, MI; Gale Research Company, 1978) and H. Colvin *Biographical Dictionary of British Architects, 1600-1840* (1978). A useful guide to the secondary literature is *Architectural Periodicals Index* (published quarterly by Royal Institute of British Architects Publications Ltd, 1974-) based on the contents of periodicals received by the Royal Institute of British Architects. Unfortunately, not many entries are of a historical nature and few, if any, concerned directly with sport. Nevertheless, with knowledge of the architect, builder of the facility appropriate information can sometimes be traced within larger, more general collections.

Sport and the Armed Services
(Also see History of Sport in Individual Communities, History of Individual Clubs, Teams and Other Institutions)

Sport has played an important role in the training and recreation of servicemen throughout history. Most branches of the armed services have extensive archives but few contain much material on sport. Most valuable for material on sport are yearbooks, autobiographies and memoirs of servicemen, a few histories of individual regiments and the numerous regimental journals, large collections of which are housed in the library of the National Army Museum (Royal Hospital Road, London, SW3 4HT, Tel: 071-730-0717). There are literally thousands of private papers of military leaders deposited in libraries and record offices throughout the UK. Occasionally their correspondence touches upon issues of physical training and recreational sport. Numerous manuals and yearbooks were published for the armed services, many of which are held at the Ministry of Defence Library (3-5 Great Scotland Yard, London, SW1 2HW, Tel: 071-218-8266). Prior permission to use the library is required and not necessarily granted. Most regiments and divisions of the armed services have their own museums and archival record collections. The Army Physical Training Corps and the Physical Training branch of the Royal Marines have valuable collections at their respective headquarters in Aldershot and Portsmouth. The Army and the RAF Sports Control Boards have minutes and various publications such as yearbooks dating from after the first world war. Much manuscript material is to be found scattered in various files at the Public Record office in Kew (see p. 39) and the India Records Office on the Strand. Many useful guides to sources and bibliographies of secondary works exist but again few include information relating specifically to sport. Even N. A. Webber's nineteen volume bibliography on the history of the RAF (Ph.D. thesis, University of London, 1976) fails to include material on sport. The use of military training and military personnel to improve the physical condition of school children was the subject of much debate and inquiry in the late nineteenth and early twentieth century. The correspondence section of *The Times* carried much material during these years and there were several parliamentary enquiries (see p.68). Useful guides to background information are A. P. C. Bruce *British Army from the Roman Invasion to the Restoration: A Bibliography* (New York: Garland, 1975) and his *A Bibliography of British Military History* (New York: Saur, 1981), Higham *Guide to British Military History* (London: RKP, 1972) and J. C. Natra *Guide to Sources of British Military History* (London: Routledge, 1971). Finally, a good deal of material on sport in the services during wartime is contained in the photographic and oral history collections of the Imperial War Museum.

Sports Coaching (See Sports Training)

Sports Costume
(Also see Artefacts, Ephemena and Sports Industry)

The enthusiasm of many young women for some form of physical exercise in the latter part of the nineteenth century played a very real part in freeing women from the more tedious of Victorian constraints, particularly as they related to dress. This has been the focus of much of the research on sporting costume in recent years.

The most comprehensive treatment of sporting costume to date is probably P. Cunningham and A. Mansfield *English Costume for Sport and Outdoor Recreation: From the Sixteenth to Nineteenth Century* (London: A. and C. Black, 1969). Occasional articles have since appeared in *Costume,* (the Journal of the History of Costume Society) and a number of fashion journals (e.g. A Costume for Oarswomen, 1919-1979, *Costume, 13 (1979)*).

In terms of primary source material, a significant number of artefacts, patterns, photographs and fashion magazines are contained in the Museum of Costume/Costume and Fashion Research Centre, (4 The Circus, Bath, BA1 2EW, Tel: 0255-461111) many municipal and specialist sports museums (mentioned on p. 47) and the collections of manufacturers of sporting equipment (mentioned on same page). Finally, a number of private individuals have built up significant collections, an example being Mr. David Patterson of Stoke on Trent who has an exclusive collection of swimming caps. Unfortunately, other than the register maintained by the Ephemera Society (see p. 48), there is no easy way of identifying such individual collectors. Specialist societies of colletors such as the Cricket Memorabilia Society and the Rugby League Collector's Federation are listed on p. 48.

The most obvious and commonly used primary sources, however, especially for earlier periods are paintings and prints (see *Costume for Sport* (The Gallery of English Costume Series No. 8), Manchester: Art Galleries Committee of the Corporation of Manchester, 1963 and p. 45).

Sport and Education (Including the History of Physical Education)
(Also see Central Government Records, History of Sport in Individual Communities and Other Institutions)

The history of sport and athletic ideals within public schools and the ancient universities has been a topic of considerable interest to several sports historians over the past few decades, for it was in these institutions that many games were transformed from rudimentary pastimes into highly structured sports.

Several studies have been made in recent years of the development of physical education within the state educational system. Such studies have often been undertaken by professional physical educationists and submitted for higher degrees within departments of education. Unfortunately, relatively few have offered in-depth scholarly analysis and it is perhaps for this reason that only a small number have ever been published. Most remain in their unpublished forms as theses and dissertations.

Sources for the history of physical education in both private and public sectors of education during the 19th and 20th centuries are many and diverse. Examples of bibliographies, bibliographical series and indexes include: J. Cragie *A Bibliography of Scottish Education Before 1872* (London: University of London Press, 1970) and its supplement 1872-1972 (1974); V. F. Gilbert and C. Holmes *Theses and Dissertations on the History of Education Presented at British and Irish Universities Between 1900 and 1976* (Leicester: History of Education Society, 1979) (with yearly supplements also published by the History of Education Society); D. G. Paz "American Dissertations on the History of British and Irish Education Completed Between 1958 and 1973', *History of Education Society Bulletin*, 13 (Spring, 1974); J. M. McCarthy *An International List of Articles on the History of Education Published in Non-Educational Journals, 1965-74* (New York: Garland, 1977); R. Szreter "The History of Education in Non-Educational Periodicals, 1937-1967: A Bibliography', *British Journal of Educational Studies*, 16 (1968).

Useful guides to local material include: P. Cunningham *Local History of Education in England and Wales: A Bibliography* (Educational Administration and History Monograph Series No. 4) (Leeds: University of Leeds Museum of the History of Education, 1974) and P. J. Wallis "Articles on the History of Education in Local Journals', *History of Education Society Bulletin*, 11 (Spring, 1973). For biographical material a highly selective and now very much dated bibliography is A. Christopher *An Index to 19th Century Educational Biography* (Education Libraries Bulletin Supplement No. 10, 1965).

There are many other guides to secondary sources focusing on specific types, levels and forms of education e.g.: H. Silver and S. J. Teague *The History of British Universities, 1800-1969: A Bibliography* (Research into Higher Education Monograph No. 13) (London: Society for Research into Higher Education, 1970); M. Berry *Teacher Training in England and Wales: A Bibliographical Guide to Their History* (Research into Higher Education Monograph No. 18) (London: Society for Research into Higher Education, 1973): P. J. Wallis *Histories of Old Schools: A Revised List for*

England and Wales (Newcastle-upon-Tyne, University of Newcastle-upon-Tyne Institute of Education, 1966). Unfortunately, to list all the many bibliographical aids would take up considerable space. Researchers are advised to consult one or more of the special collections listed below in order to compile a more detailed list. Many recent publications and much completed research is reported in *Paedogogica Historica* (published twice a year by the Centre for the Study of the History of Education, University of Ghent, since 1961) and "A Bibliography for Historians of Education' in each issue of *History of Education Quarterly* (USA). More general education current awareness services such as *British Education Index, Education Index, ERIC - CIJE*, are noted on p. 20.

For identifying primary sources W. B. Stephens *Sources for Local History* (Cambridge University Press, 1981) has a valuable chapter devoted to education and is particularly useful for sources for the history of voluntary education in the 19th century. So is W. B. Stephens and R. W. Unwin *Materials for the Local and Regional Study of Schooling, 1700-1900* (London: British Records Association, 1987). It must be remembered, however, that with few exceptions, physical training was not included in the curriculum of voluntary sector education until the present century.

A large number of guides to primary sources on specific types, levels, forms of education exist and are to be found in issues of the *History of Education Society Bulletin* (1968 onwards); the *British Journal of Educational Studies* (particularly numbers published in the 1950s and 60s) and the History of Education Society *Guide To Sources in the History of Education* series and a number of their occasional publications, the first of which (*Archives* and the *History of Education* 1975) includes a bibliographical review essay by C. Crunden on the history of elementary school physical education.

Many parliamentary papers passed comment on physical education following the formation of the Committee of Council on Education in 1839. In addition to information contained within the *Minutes of the Committee of Council* (1839/40-1857/58), later *Annual Reports of the Education Department* (1858/59-1899); Board of Education (1899/1900-1938/39), Ministry of Education (1944-63), Department of Education and Science (1964 to 1992), Department for Education (1992 to date) and the *Annual Reports of the Chief Medical Officer of the Board of Education* (1908-1939), reports of several commissions and departmental, inter-departmental enquiries commented on the physical education and training of school children. Much material on public school athleticism is contained in the report of the *Royal Commission on Public Schools* (Clarendon Commission), and even more on elementary school physical education in the *Report of the Royal Commission on Physical Training (Scotland)* 1903, and the *Report of the Inter-Departmental Report on Physical Deterioration* 1904. Many series of parliamentary and non-parliamentary papers devoted sections to physical training, for example, the Board of Education *Special Reports on Educational Subjects* (87); Board/Department of Education *Circulars,* (88) *Pamphlets* (89) and *Handbooks of Suggestions for Teachers* . (90) The Board of Education also initiated a *Physical Training Series.* (91) Considerable manuscript material on physical education is to be found in the Public Record Office (see p. 39). A most useful, but unpublished subject index to the files on education contained within the Public Record Office is held in the DFE Library.

Useful guides to parliamentary papers on education are M.V. Argles and J.E. Vaughan *British Government Papers Concerning Education: An Introductory Guide* (Liverpool: University of Liverpool Institute of Education Library, 1966) and W. B. Stephens and R. W. Unwin *Materials for the Local and Regional Study of Schooling, 1700-1900* (British Records Association, 1987). For identifying specific forms of government documents use: J. E. Vaughan *Board of Education Circulars: A Finding List and Index* (Guides to Sources in the History of Education Series), and the Librarians of Institutes and School of Education Libraries *List of Educational Pamphlets of the Board of Education 1904-1943 With Locations* (London: LISEL, 1962).

At the local level, minutes and annual reports of the School Board/Education Committee, Annual reports of the School Medical Officer and Organisers/Inspectors/Advisors reports usually carried sections on physical training. A number of districts formed school sports associations and leagues, the records of which have been deposited with the local record office. Cuttings, books and various items of ephemera relating to the activities of the Enfield School Sports Association and the Edmonton Schools FA (1920-1950s) for example, are deposited with the local history library at Enfield.

In terms of the teacher unions' point of view some interesting material on the relative merits of swedish and military forms of drill and the training of specialist physical education teachers is contained in manuscript files held by the NUT Library (Hamilton House, Mabeldon Place, London, WC1H 9BD, Tel: 071-387-2442) and publications of several other pressure groups (e.g. The Ling Association (fore runner of the Physical Education Association of Great Britain and Northern Ireland). (92)

The views of many different other groups together with those of individuals towards physical training and sport in education are expressed in the pages of the *The Times* (see D. Leinster-Mackay and E. Sarfaty *Education and the Times: An Index to Letters to 1910* (London: Mansell, 1992), *The Times Educational Supplement* (1847 to date, although the original title was *The Educational Times),* and many other organs of the teaching profession. A useful list of titles with dates is included in L. Fletcher *The Teachers' Press in Britain* (Educational Administration and History Monograph Series No. 7 (Leeds: University of Leeds Museum of the History of Education, 1978). There have been several periodicals specifically devoted to physical training, of one form or another, although most were short lived. Examples include the *Leaflet of the Ling Association* (1902-1920) and the *Journal of Scientific Physical Training* (1909-1920). Several such titles are held by the library of the Physical Education Association of Great Britain and Northern Ireland (which has recently moved from the Whitelands campus of the Roehampton Institute of Higher Education to Sheffield Sports Library) (see p. 15). A very useful subject index to a broad range of periodical publications listing many items on physical training and education is *Education Miscellanies and Pamphlets*. This was the basis of an in-house current awareness service produced for staff of the Board of Education by staff of the former Board of Education library. It is available for consultation in the DFE library. Two useful compendiums of articles on physical training in schools published during the late nineteenth and early twentieth centuries are J. Atkins (ed.) *National Physical Training* (London: Isbister and Co., 1904) and L. Brunton *Collected Papers on Physical and Military Training* (London: 1915).

Special collections of important, influential historical documents relating to education have been published (e.g. S. McClure *Educational Documents: England and Wales, 1816 to the Present Day* (London: Methuen, 1973), R.W. Unwin and W. B. Stephens *Yorkshire School and Schooldays - A Guide to Historical Sources and Their Uses* (Leeds: University of Leeds Institute of Education, 1970). Many primary sources have been reprinted in microform in the *Journal of Sources in Educational History* Volume 4, No. 1 (1982) edited by R. W. Cox is devoted exclusively to primary sources for the history of physical education.

There have not been a very large number of textbooks on Physical Education published in Britain. A useful finding aid for some of these is C. W. J. Higson *Sources for the History of Education: A List of Material (including school books) contained in the libraries of the Institutes and Schools of Education* (London: The Library Association, 1967) (Supplement 1976), although now considerably out of date.

There are several specialist education libraries in Britain. The library of the Department For Education (Sanctuary Buildings, Great Smith Street, London, SW1P 3B7, Tel: 071-925-`5011) has a collection of all official documents issued on education, including physical education. It houses the Grenfell Collection of Books on Physical Education and has an excellent collection of finding aids. Other special collections include: the library of the Museum of the History of Education, University of Leeds; The Carnegie Historical Collection of Books on Sport, Physical Education and Health Education which is held in the Beckett Park Library, Leeds Metropolitan University; (93) the library of the NUT (which holds copies of all NUT issued documents concerning education) and the libraries of several of the larger university institutes and Schools of Education libraries e.g. the University of London Institute of Education (11-13 Ridgmount Street, London, WC1E 7AH, Tel: 071-637-0846). (94)

Many sources for the history of physical education overseas also exist. For the history of education in the United States of America, F. Cardasco and W. W. Brickman *A Bibliography of American Educational History* (New York: AMS Press, 1978) is a valuable source and may be updated using some of the current awareness services already mentioned above, especially the one published in *History of Education Quarterly*. A supplement to the *Education Libraries Bulletin* compiled by M. A. Greaves and entitled *Education in British India, 1689-1947: A Bibliography and Guide to Sources of Information* will be of help to the historian of physical education in India. The University of London Institute of Education Library has a large collection of material on comparative education (and for which a dictionary catalogue was published by G. K. Hall, Boston in 1971).

Finally, mention should be made of archive collections of some of the schools. Several of the older educational establishments have maintained extensive archives, some better managed than others, which include such items as school newspapers and magazines, headmaster's diaries. Higher degree theses by J.A. Mangan and M. Tozer (95) illustrate the vast range of source material available and the nature of information it provides. Unfortunately, few state schools have very extensive archives although miscellaneous items of possible interest- registers, log books are sometimes to be found in the local record office.

Sports Equipment (See Artefacts, Sports Costume, Patents and Sports Industry)
Sports Fiction
(Also see Contemporary Literature)

The study of the history of sports fiction is a recent phenomenon. Its popularity is reflected in the formation of a Sports Literature Association (SLA) and the publication of *Aethlon* (formerly *Arete)* a scholarly international journal devoted to the study of sports literature (published in Johnson City by East Tennesse University Press for the SLA since 1984). To identify publications dealing specifically with sport there are the following bibliographies: G. Burns *The Sports Pages - A Critical Bibliography of 20th Century American Novels and Stories Featuring Baseball, Basketball, Football and Other Athletic Pursuits* (Metuchen, NY: Scarecrow Press, 1989) and S. Wise *Sports Fiction for Adults: An Annotated Bibliography* (New York: Garland Press, 1984). More general reference works include: *The New Cambridge Bibliography of English Literature* (Cambridge University Press, 1981, new version in preparation), *Essay and General Literature Index* , *English Literature Index, British Literary Bibliography, Fiction Index, Dissertations on English Literature* and the many individual bibliographies published on the works of and criticisms of the works of individual authors (e.g. D. Gerard *Alan Sillitoe: A Bibliography* London: Mansell, 1988). There are many special collections separately housed or held as part of more general collections. The Sydney Jones Library, University of Liverpool, for example, collects works on Blake whilst the University of Birmingham is home to the Shakespeare Library (for details of other special collections consult the *Aslib Guide*, etc. see p. 13). To provide details of literary manuscripts Mansell have published a four volume series covering the period 1450-1900.

Sport and Gambling
(Also see Sport and the Law)

Gambling has a long association with sport, especially horse-racing, and has been the subject of a recent book by M. Clapson *A Bit of a Flutter* (Manchester: Manchester University Press, 1992). The topic has stimulated much debate in Parliament over the years and has been the subject of several major enquiries, often resulting in the enactment of new legislation. Tracing the history of the sometimes equally well organised but illegal forms of betting that were associated with many sports from their very early days and conducted in public houses and on the streets is much more difficult. Many working-class betters and bookmakers did make court appearances and this may be one avenue to pursue. It was also a popular topic for condemnation in the sermons and published literature of the non-conformist religious groups such as the Methodists. W. Vamplew who considers the subject of gambling in great detail in his social and economic history of horse-racing *The Turf* (London: Allen Lane, 1976), quotes examples of attempts to quantify the extent of gambling in Britain in the nineteenth and twentieth centuries using information on bookmaker's taxed incomes and on the revenue raised by the betting duty with some assumptions regarding the extent of tax evasion and illegal betting only to conclude that on-one knows the true extent of the gambling that took place.

Sport and Gender

Recent years have also witnessed considerable interest in the emergent role of women in sport and the historical reasons for the nature and degree of their involvement, non-involvement. A quick reference guide to women's sporting achievements is N. McWhirter *Guinness Book of Women's Sports Records* (Enfield: Guinness Superlatives, 1979). Useful bibliographies of published works include: M. Remley *Women in Sport* (Detroit, MI: Gale, Research Co., 1980) and Michele Shoebridge *Women in Sport: A Select Bibliography* (London: Mansell, 1987). Both works provide a valuable starting point for identifying secondary literature although Shoebridge's is the more up-to-date and comprehensive guide, covering theses, dissertations, journal and some newspaper articles as well as monographs. (96)

In 1991, the *Journal of Sport History* devoted a whole issue to the theme of sport and gender.

An index to recently published scholarly works is *Studies on Women Abstracts* (published quarterly by Carfax, 1983 onwards). *Bibliofem* is a joint library catalogue and continuing bibliography of the Fawcett Library (currently based at the Guildhall University, Calcutta House, Old Castle Street, London E1 7NT) and the Equal Opportunities Commission.

Two major bibliographies of bibliographies on women's studies are P. K. Ballou *Women: A Bibliography of Bibliographies* (Boston, MA: G. K. Hall, 1986) and M. Ritchie *Women's Studies: A Checklist of Bibliographies* (London: Mansell, 1980). An index to dissertations, most of a historical nature including some on sport is V. F. Gilbert and D. S. Tatla *Women's Studies: A Bibliography of Dissertations, 1870-1982* (Oxford: Blackwell, 1985).

An important guide to manuscript sources in the UK is M. Barrow *Women 1870-1928 - Guide To Printed and Archival Sources in the UK* (London: Mansell 1981). A parallel guide to manuscript sources in the United States is A. Hinding *Women's History Sources: A Guide To Archives and Manuscript Collections in the United States* (New York: Bowker, 1979). Major archives of primary source material, including some manuscript material are the Fawcett Library (see H. L. Smith "British Women's History - The Fawcett Library's Archival Collections', *20th Century British History*, 2, 2 (1991), 215-223.) and the Feminist Archive (Trinity Road Library, Trinity Road, St Philips, Bristol, BS2 ONW).

A specialist biographical dictionary is A. Crawford *Europa Biographical Dictionary of British Women* (London: Europa Publications, 1983). This provides a collection of short biographies of notable women throughout British history.

Although 'men studies' is beginning to emerge as an area of study in some quarters, it was not considered necessary to discuss it as a separate issue here.

Sports Industry
(Also see Artefacts, Patents, Special Communities, Clubs, Teams, etc.)

Sources for the history of sport related industries are the same as for other business histories. Useful guides to source material are: J. Armstrong and S. Jones *Business Documents: Their Origins, Sources and Uses in Historical Research* (London: Mansell, 1987) and J. Orbell *A Guide To Tracing the History of a Business* (Aldershot: Gower, 1987). Between them, these two guides provide illustration of the different documents produced within business firms - such as board minutes, correspondence, balance sheets, staff records, Chairman reports, indicate where such records might be found (other than with the domestic records of the firm - e.g. the Public Record Office, Companies House, newspaper and trade journals, etc.), the information each type of record contains, the possibilities of linkage with other records and its value to the historian. Mention has already been made of individual sports clubs (p. 58) and venues (p. 61) that were registered companies and their records. Although many of the records are of a formal nature relating to the business of the company as a company, registers of shareholders, ledgers, wage books, etc can enable the pattern of ownership and the financial affairs of the syndicate to be analysed.

Unfortunately, of the many bibliographies of business histories and business archives published in recent years (e.g. F. Goodall *A Bibliography of British Business Histories* (Aldershot: Gower, 1987) and L. Richmond and B. Stockford *Company Archives - The Survey of the Records of 1,000 of the First Registered Companies in England and Wales* (Aldershot: Gower, 1986), none examined by the author has been found to list any of sporting organisations. Records of sports related business are, however, to be found in record offices throughout the UK The records of Lanark Racecourse Company, for example, are held in Glasgow University Archives. A useful starting place to identify the whereabouts of company records is the NRA (see pp. 27-28). The files of defunct companies are kept by the Register of Companies until they are about twenty years old when they are transferred to the Public Record Office. The files of dissolved companies are located in the PRO Classes BT 41 and BT 31 (for companies disolved after the 1860s); in the Scottish Record Office in Class BT 2 and in the Public Record Office of Northern Ireland in class COM 90. An article by J. R. Lowerson entitled "A Little Used Source for Sports Historians - Limited Liability Company Records', *British Society of Sports History Bulletin*, 7 (1987) discusses the contents of Board of Trade files within the Public Records Office and an article by A. J. Arnold "The Belated Entry of Professional Soccer into the West Riding Textile District of Northern England: Commercial Imperatives and Problems', *International Journal of the History of Sport*, 6, 3 (December,1989), 319-334, illustrates, by way of example, how these records can be put to good use in historical research.

Directories, sports trade magazines, catalogues of equipment, price lists and advertisements can sometimes be helpful sources as reflected in the volume on *Nineteenth Century Games and Sporting Goods* in the *American Historical Catalog Collection* (Princeton, NJ: The Pyne Press, n.d.). Large shops, especially those with a mail order service regularly published catalogues. The Sports and Games Department section of the *Get It At Harrods* catalogue usually ran to several pages. Manufacturers, wholesalers and retailers dealing in bicycles generated many such publications. Unfortunately, bibliographical control of these types of publication is non-existent and there are few special collections known to the author. The Manchester Metropolitan University library has a small collection and there may be others. The BP Library of Motor Sports (see p. 15) holds a great deal of material of interest to those researching the history of the motor car industry.

Advertisements can be a useful source of information indicating specific markets targeted and images portrayed. There are many held by the History of Advertising Trust (30 Charing Cross Road, London, WC2H OBD, Tel: 071-379-3565) depicting sport. S. A. G. M. Crawford has recently assessed the D'Arcy collection of advertisements deposited at the University of Illinois at Urbana - Champaign, as a source of information for the sports historian and found it to be most valuable (*NASSH Proceedings*, 1991, pp. 23-24).

A number of general and specialist sports museums have interesting items of clothing and equipment in their collections (see p. 47) and as also mentioned on p. 47, several manufacturers have their own historical collections of products they manufactured and tools and machines they used. Many new items of equipment, especially revolutionary designs, had patents taken out by their designers and inventors which provide important technical information as well as details of their designer and date of production (see pp. 49-50).

Sports Journalism (inc. Broadcasting)
(Also see Periodical Articles (inc Newspapers), Films, Videos and Oral Evidence.)

In addition to the sources for newspaper articles, films, etc. already outlined, *The Times*, has its own extensive archive (214 Gray Inn Road, London, WC1X 8EZ, Tel: 071-833-7346) which reflects company policy towards sport. In a similar but smaller collection, *The Guardian* archive held in the John Rylands University Library Manchester, includes considerable manuscript material, in particular exchanges of correspondence between members of the newspaper staff. Of potential value to sports historians, but so far untapped, are letters and notes by the famous cricket and music correspondent Neville Cardus (1936-56 Ref. B/C34/1-441).

The BBC Written Archives Centre, (Caversham Park, Reading) contains the correspondence records of the BBC which include dealings with sports bodies and venues for BBC coverage of sporting events (e.g. Wimbledon, Aintree). There is material for both television and radio. There is also some correspondence with sports personalities and some internal BBC papers outlining policy on certain sports. There are no scripts of actual running commentaries on sporting events, but there are scripts of BBC news bulletins which contain many references to sport. The Centre also maintains a collection of newspaper cuttings relating to BBC coverage of sport. For historians specifically interested in the history of sports broadcasting B. MacDonald *Broadcasting in the U.K: A Guide to Information Sources* (London: Mansell, 1988) is a useful guide. For those interested in the growth of the sporting press itself, D. Linton and R. Boston *The Newspaper Press in Britain: An Annotated Bibliography* (London: Mansell, 1987) may be of some help in identifying background secondary material. Finally, L. Shelton-Caswell *Guide to Sources in American Journalism History* is pertinent to those researching into the history of sports journalism in North America.

Sport and Organised Labour

S. G. Jones in his *Sport, Politics and the Working Class: Organised Labour and Sport in Inter-War Britain* (Manchester: Manchester University Press, 1988), analyses the attitude of organised labour groups to sport and in so doing reveals the vast scope of source material for the history of sport in the Labour Party and the TUC archives.

Large collections of records of labour organisations are held in the Modern Records Office at the University of Warwick Library (see: J. Bennett *Trade Union and Related Records* (5th edition) (University of Warwick Library, 1988) and at the National Museum of Labour History (103, Princess Street, Manchester M1 6DD). Some collections contain a surprising amount of material specifically on sport. Simon Fowler has recently produced a general guide to *Sources for Labour History* (Kew: Labour Heritage, 1991) and the Society for the Study of Labour History has produced a number of more specialist guides. *A Guide to the Labour Party Archives* complied by Stephen Bird was published by the organisation in 1983. Reviews of labour archieves were published in *Archivum* 27 (1980) and *Labour History Review* 57 (Spring, 1992).

A valuable collection of Labour Party news cuttings and pamphlets is held in the John Rylands University Library, Manchester. A cursory scan of the in-house index to the collection reveals a significant amount of material relating to sport. Several organised labour movements still house their own records, an example being the Professional Footballer's Association. Stored at their headquarters in Manchester, these records were extensively used by John Harding in his history of that organisation (*More Than A Game: The Official History of the PFA* London: Robson, 1991). The records of teachers' unions towards physical education are discussed on p. 68.

Many politically motivated pamphlets and leaflets produced by such bodies as the Conservative and Unionist Party and the British Trade Union Congress have been reproduced on microfilm in the *Harvester Library of British Political Pamphlets, 1868-1975*.

Sport and the Law
(Also see Legal Records)

In May 1993, a British Society for Sport and Law was founded in Manchester. This reflects a growing interest in what is emerging as a specialised field of law as sports stadia are subject to more rigorous regulations regarding safety standards at grounds (see p. 66), professional sportsmen and women involved in more complex contracts regarding the terms of their employment, different user groups fighting over access to limited resources such as moorland and waterways.

The association of Law and Sport, however, extends to much earlier times. Mention has already been made of the Game Laws of the seventeenth century, legislation regarding gambling, civil order and the playing of sports on the Sabbeth.

In addition to parliamentary debates and reports of committees of enquiry (see pp. 36-38), court records (see p. 50) and company records (see pp. 73-74) are perhaps the most fruitful sources to explore. There are numerous published bibliographies such as A. G. Chloros (ed.) *Bibliographical Guide to the Law of the United Kingdon* (2nd edition) (London: Institute of Advanced Legal Studies, University of London, 1973); indexes such as the *Legal Bibliography Index* (Louisiana State University, 1979-) and on-line services such as *LEXIS* (London: Butterwaths, 1980) a database on case and statute law.

Sports Medicine
(Also see Sports Training)

Sport and physical education have a long association with the medical profession. Support for public provision of sporting facilities was often secured on grounds of improving the nation's health. A useful source of information for those interested in the history of sports medicine is the library of the Welcome Institute for the History of Medicine (183 Euston Road, London, NW1 2AP, Tel: 071-611-8888). This large valuable and well catalogued archive has a library of secondary works and the private papers of many well known physicians, some of whom had an interest in physical development and training (e.g. the papers of Dr. Allan Broman a Swedish pioneer of medical gymnastics in England in the late 19th century).

Little, however, has so far been written on the history of sports medicine in Britain, at least as reflected in the contents of many indexes and bibliographies searched by the author, including the highly comprehensive *Bibliography of the History of Medicine* and *Current Work in the History of Medicine*. Park has stressed the importance of researching contemporary theories of biological thought, eugenics and evolution in order to understand the background to the history of physical education (see p. 1). Hopefully, this avenue of research will be tackled more thoroughly in the future, in which case new sources may well be revealed. A new resource centre which may be able to assist the researcher identify recently published secondary sources on the history of sports medicine, is the library of the London Sports Medicine Institute (c/o St. Bartholomew's Hospital, Charterhouse Square, London, EC1M 6BQ, Tel: 071-251-0583). Clinics specialising in sports injuries sometimes maintain databases containing information on the number, type, background, duration and treatment of sports injuries which may, under certain conditions, be made accessible to the bona fide researcher.

Sport and Politics
(Also see Parliamentary Papers and Reports, Sporting Festivals, History of Sport and Organised Labour)

The relationship between sport and politics at local, national and international levels has intensified in recent years. This fact has been reflected in the dramatic increase in related literature and television documentary programmes.

Although the sport historian can readily document various affinitives between sport and politics since the civilisation of the ancient world, sport has been traditionally viewed as an apolitical institution to which the addition of political considerations was undesirable. Today, it would be naive to ignore the increasing interaction between the two agents. Apart from mentioning L. Burgener et. al. "Sport and Politics: A Select Bibliography', *Cultures*, IV, 2 pp. 2-51, all other secondary and primary sources for the investigation of this subject have already been discussed.

Sports Training
(Also see Sports Medicine)

Apart from an article by P. F. Radford "The Art and Science of Training and Coaching Athletics in Late 18th and Early 19th Century Britain', *Proceedings of the XI HISPA Congress, Glasgow, 1985* pp. 80-82, an anthology of essays edited by J. W. Berryman and R. J. Park *(Sport and Exercise Science: Essays in the History of Sports Medicine,* Urbana, Il: University of Illinois Press, 1992) and the proceedings of the 63rd Annual Congress of the American Academy of Physical Education devoted to *Enhancing Human Performance in Sport,* there appears to have been little reported research on the history of preparation and training for sporting competition.

This is surprising bearing in mind the importance attached to the subject by athletes, coaches and teachers of sport. Although one could identify books and articles which discuss contemporary theories of exercise science (in earlier sections) there would appear to be little record of coaches or mentors preparing the mind, communicating with and motivating athletes prior to the 19th century. Some clues may be gleaned from such sources as diaries, paintings, equipment and clothing.

References

(1)   Strutt, J., *The Sports and Pastimes of the People of England*: (London: White, 1801).

(2)   Mandell, R., *Sport: A Cultural History* (New York: Columbia University Press, 1984), p. xix. Similarly, Guttmann (A. Guttmann, *A Whole New Ball Game: An Interpretation of American Sports* (London: University of North Carolina Press, 1988), p. 21 described most sports biographies as 'exercises in hagiography or public relations rather than scholarly assessments'.

(3)   Historians have come to realise that sport in itself is capable of structuring class and gender relations within communities and even influencing the economy. They have stopped treating sport as a separate category of life apart from employment, the urban environment, and other important phenomena impinging upon human nature.

To understand sport in relation to Victorian religion, philosophy and physiology historians have drawn upon the writings of biologists, such as Sir Charles Bell and Thomas Huxley, and the 'Muscular Christian' novels of Charles Kingsley and Thomas Hughes. (See Bruce Haley *The Healthy Body and Victorian Culture* (London: Harvard University Press, 1978)). They have also made use of anthropological and sociological categories such as emulation, distancing, symbol, and ritual, cohesion and identity (see for example J. A. Mangan *Athleticism in the Victorian and Edwardian Public School* (Cambridge: Cambridge University Press, 1980).

(4)   Baker, W. B., "The Leisure Revolution in Victorian England: A Review of Recent Literature', *Journal of Sport History*, 6, 3 (Winter, 1979), p. 79.

(5)   See R. J. Holt, *Sport and the British* (Oxford: Clarendon, 1989), p. 3.

(6)   See, for example, J. J. Bagley *Historical Interpretations - Volume Two Sources of English History, 1500 to the Present Day* (Newton Abbot: David and Charles, 1972) and W. B. Stephens *Sources for English Local History* (2nd edition) (Cambridge: Cambridge University Press, 1981). Between them, these two publications contain helpful guides to and discussions of primary sources for information on a whole range of topics including agriculture, education, religion, local government, trade and industry but nothing o leisure or more specifically sport.

(7)   National Register of Archives, *Survey of Historical Manuscripts in the UK: A Select Bibliography* (London: HMSO, 1988).

(8)   Park, R. J., "Physiologists, Physicians and Physical Educators: Nineteenth Century Biology and Exercise, Hygiene and Education', *Journal of Sport History*, 14, 1 (Spring, 1987), 28-60.

(9)   Sandiford, K. A. P., "Victorian Cricket Technique and Industrial Technology', *British Journal of Sports History*, 1, 3 (December, 1984), 272-285.

(10)   Brailsford, D. W., "Religion and Sport in 18th Century England: For the Encouragement of Piety and Virtue and for the Preventing of Vice, Profoness and Immorality', *British Journal of Sports History*, 1, 2 (September, 1984), 166-183.

(11)   Fairs, J. R., "Sociocultural Control of the Body in Western Society: An Ethnioeconomic Interpretation', *Canadian Journal of the History of Sport and Physical Education*, VII, 2 (December 1976), 1-25.

(12)   Vamplew, W., *Pay Up and Play the Game: Professional Sport in Britain, 1875-1914* (Cambridge: Cambridge University Press, 1989).

(13)   The 'antiquarian' or 'chronologer' is usually primarily interested in documenting factual information such as details of results, scores, events and personalities in order to trace the major changes and turning points in the development of a particular institution. For a discussion of the scholarship and different approaches to sports history see: W. J. Baker "The State of British Sports History', *Journal of Sports History*, 10, 1 (Spring, 1983), 53-66; J. W. Berryman "Sport History as Social History', *Quest*, XX, (June, 1983), 65-73; M. L. Howell "Towards a History of Sport', *Canadian Journal of the History of Sport and Physical Education*, 1, 1 (May, 1970), 8-16; J. M. Leiper "A Survey of History of Olympism in North America', *Proceedings of International Congress on Physical Activity Sciences*, Quebec, 1976; A. Metcalfe "North American Sports History: A Review of North American Sports Historians and Their Works', *Exercise and Sports Science*

Review, 2 (1974), 225-238; A. Metcalfe "Hypothetical Versus Descriptive Sports History: An Analysis of Methodological Approaches to Sports History', *Proceedings of the VI HISPA Congress*, Dartford (April, 1977), pp. 429-438; R. J. Park "The Use of Hypotheses in Sports History', in R. Day and P. Lindsay (eds.), *Sport History Methodology*, Proceedings of a Workshop held at the University of Alberta (May/June, 1980), pp. 25-36, R. J. Park "Research and Scholarship in the History of Physical Education and Sport: The Current State of Affairs', *Research Quarterly*, 54, 2 (1983), 93-103 and "Sports History in the 1990's: Prospects and Problems' *American Academy of Physical Education Papers*, 20, (1986), 96-108; Park, R. J., "The Second Hundred Years: Or, Can Physical Education Become the Renaissance Field of the 21st Century', *Quest*, 41 (1989), 107-127. G. Redmond "Sport History in Academe - Reflections on Half a Century of Peculiar Progress', *British Journal Sports History*, 1, 1 (May, 1984), 5-13; K. A. P. Sandiford "The Victorians at Play: Problems in Historiography and Methodology', *Journal of Social History*, 15, 3 (Winter, 1981), 271-88; K. A. P. Sandiford "Cricket and the Victorians: A Historiographical Essay', *Historical Reflections*, 9 (1982), 421-436; N. Struna "In Glorious Disarray: The Literature of American Sports History', *Research Quarterly*, 56, 2 (June, 1986), 151-160 and J. Walvin "Sport, Social History and History', *The British Journal of Sports History*, 1, 1 (May, 1984), 24-40; E. F. Zeigler "Biased View of History, Historiography and Physical Education and Sport', *Proceedings of the First Canadian Symposium on the History of Sport* Edmonton (1970), pp. 625-643.

(14)   McAloon, J. J., *The Great Symbol: Pierre de Coubertin and the Origins of the Modern Olympic Games* (Chicago: University of Chicago Press, 1981).

(15)   Howell, M. L., "Archaeological Evidence of Sports and Games in Ancient Civilisations', *Canadian Journal of the History of Sport and Physical Education*, 2, 1 (May, 1971), 14-30 and 2, 2 (December, 1971), 5-29.

(16)   Vamplew, W., *Pay Up and Play the Game: ibid.*

(17)   Paddick, R. J., "Philosophy in the History of Sport and Physical Education', *Canadian Journal of the History of Sport and Physical Education*, 1, 2 (December, 1970), 4-6.

(18)   Metcalfe, A., "The Use of Psycho-Sociological Models in the Analysis of Historical Data With Special Reference to the History of Physical Activity in Canada', *Proceedings of the 74th Meeting of the National College Physical Education Association*, Portland (December, 1970), 146-150.

(19)   Bale, J. R., "Geographical Diffusion and the Adaptation of Professionalism in Football in England and Wales', *Geography*, 68 (July, 1978), 158-197.

(20)   Redmond, G., "Moral Tales for Christian Sport in Children's Literature, 1788-1857' in J.A. Mangan (ed.), *Society, Religion and Sport*, Proceedings of the British Society of Sports History, University of Keele (September, 1983), pp. 65-77.

(21)   Ingham, A. G., "Max Weber's Legacy and the Historical Study of Sport', *NASSH Proceedings* 1976, p. 42 and M. Zechetmayr "Research Methodology in Sociology as Applicable to Sport History', in R. Day and P. Lindsay *Sport History Research Methodology*, Proceedings of a workshop held at the University of Alberta (May/June, 1980), pp. 140-151.

(22)   A 5th edition of Walford is currently in preparation. Volume 1 - *Science and Technology* published in 1989. Volume 2 - *Social and Historical Sciences* published in 1990.

(23)   For specifically sports biographical dictionaries see pp. 61-63.

(24)   See for example: P. Lovesey and T. McNab (eds.), *A Guide to Track and Field Literature, 1275-1968* (London: Athletics Arena, 1969), Mallon, B., *The Olympics: A Bibliography* (New York: Garland, 1984), R. W. Cox "Publications on the History of Sport in the North West (Cheshire, Cumbria and Lancashire)', *Proceedings of One Day Workshop on the History of Sport in the North West*, University of Lancaster (July, 1987). L. G. Davies, *Joe Louis: A Bibliography of Articles, Books, Pamphlets, Records and Archival Materials* (Westport, CT: Greenwood Press, 1983), T. F. Scanlon *Greek and Roman Athletics: A Bibliography* (Chicago, IL: Aires Press, 1984), R. W. Cox, "Annual Bibliography of Publications on the History of Sport 1985/6', *British Journal of Sport History*, 4, 3 (December, 1987), 351-359, M. Shoebridge *Women in Sport: A Select Bibliography* (London: Mansell, 1987), R. W. Cox (comp.), *Theses and Dissertations on the History of Sport, Physical Education and Recreation Accepted for Higher Degrees and Advanced Diplomas in British Universities, 1900-1981* (Liverpool: Bibliographical Centre for the History

of Sport and Physical Education, 1982), *Catalogue of the Alpine Club Library* (London, The Alpine Club, 1982), Recent Publications by Members (Published periodically in the HISPA Bulletin, Dickinson, J., *An Annotated Bibliography of Historical Writings Related to Physical Education in National Professional Physical Education Journals and Proceedings in North America in the Last Decade,* M. S. thesis, University of Oregon, 1973, G. Bridge, *Rock Climbing in the British Isles 1894-1970: A Bibliography of Guide Books* Reading: West Cal Publications, 1971).

(25)   There is considerable overlap between different indexing and abstracting services. J. Lingenfelter et.al. in a comparison of five Physical Education Indexing/Abstracting services (R. Q, 21, (1981), pp. 53-60), for example, found 70% overlap between *Physical Education Index* and *Physical Education/Sports Index.* There are ,however, some important sports periodicals not indexed in either one. For a more detailed discussion see R. W. Cox "Subject Bibliographies', *British Journal of Academic Librarianship* 7, 1 (1992) 17-29.

(26)   A supplement to cover the period 1979-1989 compiled by S. Eley was published by the Library Association in June, 1991, a further supplement is in preparation.

(27)   See: L. Sawula *Repository of Primary and Secondary Sources for Canadian History of Sport and Physical Education* (Halifax, Nova Scotia: Dalhousie University School of Physical Education, 1974). A listing of primary and secondary material of interest to sports historians found in over forty Canadian Libraries and Research Centre.

(28)   R.K. Barney *A Source Bibliography - the History of Sport and Physical Education* (London, Ontario: University of Western Ontario, 1979), A list of more than one thousand books from the Weldon Library published between 1889 and 1979.

(29)   See: L. H. Wright *Sporting Books in the Huntington Library* (Saint Marino, CA: The Huntington Library, 1937).

(30)   See for example L. R. Albee *The Bartlett Collection: A List of Books on Angling, Fishes and Fish Culture* in the *Harvard University Library Bibliographical Contributions Series* No. 51 (1896).

(31)   The New York Public Library has from time to time published check lists of books on specific sporting topics in its *Bulletin,* see for example; "A Bibliography of Boxing: A Chronological Checklist of Books Published in England before 1900', *New York Public Library Bulletin,* 52, 6 (June, 1948), pp. 263-286; "The Spalding Baseball Collection', *New York Public Library Bulletin,* 26, 1 (January 1922), pp. 86-127 and "List of Works Relating to Fishing', *New York Public Library Bulletin,* 13, 4 (April, 1909), pp. 259-307.

(32)   See J. P. Tuck "Sources for the History of Popular Culture in the John Rylands University Library of Manchester', *Bulletin of the John Rylands University Library Manchester,* 71, 2 (Summer, 1989), 159-180.

(33)   See the *Dictionary Catalogue of the Applied Life Studies Library* (four vols) (Boston, MA: G. K. Hall, 1977)

(34)   See the *Dictionary Catalogue of the Library of Sports in the Racquets and Tennis Club, New York, With Special Collections on Tennis, Lawn Tennis and Early American Sport* (two vols) (Boston, MA: G. K. Hall, 1970).

(35)   See N. D. Cleland *Selected Sports Book Reviewing Between 1970 and 1980,* Doctoral dissertation, University of Tennessee, Knoxville, 1982 and "Comparison of Sports Coverage in *Book Review Digest* and *Book Review Index" R.Q.,* 23, 4 (Summer, 1984), pp. 451-459.

(36)   See the list of journals publishing sports history articles in D. Booker *Directory of Scholars Identifying With the History of Sport* (4th edition) (Pennsylvannia: North American Society of Sports Historians, 1988), pp. 75-76.

(37)   Lake, F. and Wright H., *A Bibliography of Archery* (Manchester: Simon Archery Foundation, 1974), p. 324.

(38)   Little, A., *Catalogue of the Kenneth Ritchie Library* (London, 1982), pp. 35-47.

(39)   *The Cricketer,* for the years 1921-60 has been indexed by H. A. Cohen in The *Journal of the Cricket Society* vol. I, 1, 53-64; I, 2, 56-60; I, 3, 57-64; II, 1, 57-64; II, 2, 61-72; II, 3, 53-64; III, 3, 59-63; III, 4, 61-64; The *Cricket Statistician,* for the years 1973-1981 (Issues 1-77) has been indexed by L. J. Newell (Retford: Association of Cricket Statisticians, n.d.) and Volumes I to IV of The *Journal of the Cricket Society* are indexed in volume V of the Journal itself. For a useful guide to cricket indexes, bibliographies see D.

R. Allen *Catalogue of Cricket Catalogues, Booklists, Bibliographical Sources and Indexes etcetera* ibid.

(40) Other indexing and abstracting periodicals, plus more detailed information about some of the ones listed (e.g. how they might be accessed, charges, etc.) may be found in directories such as the *KWIC Index to English Language Abstracting and Indexing Publications Currently Being Received by the British Library Document Supply Centre* (Boston Spa: British Library Document Supply Centre, published periodically).

(41) J. Lingenfelter, et al., compared five physical education indexing and abstracting services: *Completed Research in Health, Physical Education, Recreation and Dance, Physical Education Index, Physical Education/Sport Index, Sociology of Leisure Abstracts* (now *Sport and Leisure*), *Sport and Recreation Index* (now *Sports Search*) and *Sports Documentation Monthly Bulletin*. The researchers found a 70% overlap between *Physical Education Index* and *Physical Education/Sport Index, R.Q.* 21, (1981), pp. 53-60. A year later, V. S. Sharma analysed the contents of selected on-line sports databases, *Database* (August, 1982), pp. 32-46.

(42) T. Mason in his *Association Football and English Society, 1836-1915* (Brighton: Harvester Press, 1980), W. J. Murray in *The Old Firm: Sectarianism and Sport in Scotland* (Edinburgh: John Donald, 1984) and R. J. Holt in *Sport and Society in Modern France* (London: Macmillan, 1981) all note suspicion on the part of the club officials to outside inquiries.

(43) This series was reprinted in the 1980s by Ashford of Southampton. For a discussion of the historical importance of this influential series see: A. Briggs "The View From Badminton' in A. Briggs (ed.), *Essays in the History of Publishing in Celebration of the 250th Anniversary of the House of Longmans, 1724-1974* (London: Longmans, 1974), pp. 187-218. In this article, the author discusses the relationship between sport and society as reflected through this influential series.

(44) See the Pavilion Library Series of cricket classics.

(45) Eisen, G., "Physical Activity, Physical Education and Sport in the Old Testament', *Canadian Journal of the History of Sport and Physical Education*, VI, 2 (December, 1985), 44-65.

(46) T. Moore in the *British Society of Sport History Bulletin*, 9, (1990), 73-79.

(47) Parsons, A., *Durham City Cricket Club History* (Darlington: Durham City Cricket Club, 1980), p. 7.

(48) Carr, R., *English Fox-Hunting: A History* (London: Weidenfeld and Nicholson, 1976), p. xv.

(49) See R. Le Blancq, et. al. "Sports, Leisure and Recreation Information on the New York Times Database', *Database*, (August, 1982), pp. 52-53.

(50) See *The International Journal of the History of Sport*, 5, 1 (May, 1988), p. 158.

(51) See *American Periodicals: An Index to Microform Collections and Serials in Microform*.

(52) See for example: C. Veitch "Play Up, Play Up and Win the War: Football, the Nation and the First World War', *Journal of Contemporary History*, 20, 3 (July, 1985), pp. 363-378 and G. Redmond "Moral Tales for Manly Boys: Christian Sport in Children's Literature 1783-1857', in J. A. Mangan (ed.), *Religion, Society and Sport*, Proceedings of the Inaugural Conference of the British Society of Sports History, University of Keele (September, 1983), pp. 65-77.

(53) Orme, N. I., *Early British Swimming, 55 BC to AD1719* (Exeter: University of Exeter Press, 1983).

(54) See for example M. Tozer's Physical Education at Thring's Uppingham, M.Ed. Thesis, University of Leicester, 1974.

(55) See the *Catalogue of the Columbia University Oral History Collection* (to date six vols published by Meckler).

(56) See P. M. King's Guide to *Transcripts of the Black Women's Oral History Project* (London: Meckler, 1986).

(57) See for example: S. F. Caldwell's "Oral History - New Horizons for Physical Education and Sports Historians', *Proceedings of the National College Physical Education Association*, San Diego (December, 1966); S. A. Davidson "Oral History - Gimmickry or Valid Research?' in R. Day and P. Lindsay *Sports History Research Methodology* Proceedings of a Workshop held at the University of Alberta (May/June, 1980) pp. 62-72, B. Schrodt "Oral History in Sports History Research', also in Day and Lindsay pp. 73-76, M. Trekell "Learning to Listen - Listening to Learn: Innovations in Oral History', *Proceedings of the First World Symposium on the History of Sport and Physical Education*, Wingate Institute, Israel (1972), pp. 21-1 - 21-8.

(58)   Streeton, R., *P. G. H. Fender, A Biography* (London: Faber and Faber, 1981), p 7.

(59)   Baker, W. J., *Jesse Owens: An American Life* (New York: Free Press, 1986).

(60)   See R. G. Osterhovot "Sports History Through Art', *Journal of Health, Physical Education and Recreation*, 49, (June, 1978), 66; B. J. Putman "Art in Historical Research', *Canadian Journal of the History of Sport and Physical Education*, 1, 2 (December, 1970), pp. 52-69; H. L. Ray "History of Sport as Expressed in Art Forms', *Proceedings of the 2nd World Symposium on the History of Sport and Physical Education*, Banff (May/June, 1971); pp. 45-48 and M. Rousey "A History of Sport Through the Media of Art', *Proceedings of the National College Physical Education Association* (1966), pp. 27-29.

(61)   Mason, A., *Sport in Britain* (London: Faber and Faber, 1988), pp. 46-59.

(62)   Ford, J., *This Sporting Land* (London: New English Library, 1976), p. 128.

(63)   Henderson, T. and Stirk, D. I., *Golf in the Making* (Bradford: The Authors, 1979), pp. 299-309.

(64)   Parry, N. A., *The Liverpool Gymnasium*, M. Ed. Thesis, University of Manchester, 1974.

(65)   Pritchard, D. M. C., *A History of Croquet* (London: Cassell, 1986), p. 239.

(66)   See D. Q. Voit "Essaying the History of a Single Sport', in R. Day and P. Lindsay *Sport History Research Methodology* (1980) ibid. pp. 37-45.

(67)   Also see sections on manuscripts, sport in individual communities, history of individual sporting competitions, etc.)

(68)   See for example, J. A. Mangan *The Games Ethic and Imperialism* (Harmonsworth: Viking, 1986), *Sport: The Cultural Bond* (London: Frank Cass, 1992); A. Mason "Some Englishmen and Scotsmen Abroad: The Spread of World Football', in A. Tomlinson and G. Whannel *Off the Ball* (London: Pluto, 1986), pp. 67-82 and G. Redmond *Sporting Scots of Nineteenth Century Canada* (East Brunswick, NJ: Farleigh Dickinson University Press, 1983).

(69)   See E. Asare The Impact of British Colonialisation on the Development of Education and Physical Education in Ghana, Ph.D. Thesis, University of Leicester, 1982.

(70)   Bailey, P. C., *Leisure and Class in Victorian England* (London: R.K.P., 1978).

(71)   Meller, H., *Leisure and the Changing City, 1870-1914I*(London: R. K. P., 1976).

(72)   Metcalfe, A., "Organised Sport in the Mining Communities of South Northumberland, 1800-1889', *Victorian Studies*, 25, 4 (Summer, 1982), 469-495.

(73)   See for example: J. B. Oxendine *American Indian Sports Heritage* (Champaign, IL: Human Kinetics, 1988); M.A. Salter *Games of the Australian Aborigine*, M.A. Thesis, University of Alberta, 1967; M. A. Salter's Games in Ritual: A Study of Selected North American Indian Tribes, Ph. D. thesis, University of Alberta, 1971; C. Tatz *Aborigines in Sport* (Adelaide: Australian Society for Sports History, 1987). D. Wiggins "From Plantation to Playing Field: Historical Writings on the Black Athlete in American Sport', *Research Quarterly*, 57, 2 (June, 1986), 101-106.

(74)   Wigglesworth, N., *A Social History of Rowing in England From 1715 to the Present Day*, Ph. D. Thesis, University of Manchester, 1988, p. 283. In researching his social history of rowing, Wigglesworth found examples of club records lost (Shrewsbury Rowing Club), burnt (Gravesend R.C.), destroyed by flooding (York City R.C.), withheld as confidential (Leander R.C.).

(75)   For an illustration of the kind of information that can be gleaned from club minutes see S. Archdale "Ewhurst Cricket Club Minute Book', *The Cricketer*, 71, 8 (March, 1990), 40-41.

(76)   See for example: M. L. and R. A. Howell "The Olympic Movement Restored: The 1908 Games' in F. Landry and W. A. R. Orban (eds.) *Philosophy, Theology and the History of Sport and Physical Activity* (Quebec: Symposia Specialists, 1978), pp. 317-326; R. Mechlikoff and P. Lupcho "The Emergence of the Cold War Olympics: London 1948' in the *Proceedings of the 4th Canadian Symposium on the History of Sport and Physical Education*, University of British Columbia (June, 1979).

(77)   See M. Brickford *Avery Brundage Collection 1908-1975* (Koln: Verlag Hofmann Schorndorf, 1977).

(78)   For discussion of biographical research see: F.Cosentino "The Use of Biography as an Instrument in Sports History', in R. Day and P. L. Lindsay (eds.), *Sports History Research Methodology* Proceedings of a Workshop held at the University of Alberta (May/June, 1980), pp. 51-54 and J. A. Lucas "Sports History Through Biography', *Quest*, 31, 2 (1979), pp. 216-221 and D. Morrow "Biographical Studies' in R. D. Day

and P. L. Lindsay (1980) ibid. pp. 55-61. For discussion of methodological issues in sports biography see K. Moore "Two Methodological Problems in Biographical research - A Personal Reflection' in R. Day and P. Lindsay (eds.) (1980), ibid. pp. 122-128.

(79)   R. Carr, for example, found the *Dictionary of National Biography* to be 'notoriously weak on fox-hunting worthies'.

(80)   C. J. Bartlett has compiled a guide to to "First Class Cricketers Appearing in "Who Was Who', 1897-1970', in the *Journal of the Cricket Society*, 9, 3 (Autumn, 1979), pp. 42-45 and 9, 4 (Spring, 1980), 72-75

(81)   Those interested in university and college sport may find the following sources helpful: M. Johnston "Bibliography of the Registers (Printed) of the Universities, Inns of Court, Colleges and Schools of Great Britain and Ireland' *Bulletin of the Institute of Historical Research*, 10 (1932) pp. 109-113.

(82)   For further details and other examples see H. J. Hanham "Some Neglected Sources of Biographical Information -County Biographical Dictionaries, 1890-1937', *Bulletin of the Institute of Historical Research*, XXXIV (1961).

(83)   See for example: Paviere *A Dictionary of Sporting Painters* (Lewis, 1980), C. Martin-Jenkins *The Complete Who's Who of Test Cricketers* (London: Orbis, 1980); P. Joannou *Who's Who of Newcastle United* (Newcastle-Upon-Tyne: Newcastle United Supporters Club, 1983), *Encyclopaedia of Jews in Sport*; L. Stapleton "First Class Cricketing Old Blues', *Journal of the Cricket Society*, 10, 3 (Autumn, 1981), pp. 33-37, and 10, 4 (Spring, 1982), pp. 11-14, etc.

(84)   See J. B. Moore *Joe Dimaggio: A Bio-Bibliography* (Westport, CT: Greenwood Press, 1986)

(85)   For a fine example of how interview techniques have been used in a biographical study see W. J. Baker *Jesse Owens: An American Life* (London: Collier Macmillan, 1986).

(86)   See the five vol. *Index to Portraits in the National Portrait Gallery* (London: National Portrait Gallery) and R. Ormond and M. Rogers' *Dictionary of British Portraiture* (London: Batsford, 1981). The first comprehensive handbook of portraits of famous British Men and Women and details of where to find the portraits.

(87)   For example Volume Two contains several articles on sport and physical training under School Boards in different parts of the country. Volume Six includes an article on physical training in private preparatory schools.

(88)   For example Board of Education Circular - 1601, 10 August, 1942, *Equipment for Games and Physical Training* (London: HMSO)

(89)   For example Board of Education Education Pamphlet-No 80, 1930 *School Playing Fields* (London: HMSO)

(90)   For example Board of Education, *Suggestions for the Consideration of Teachers* (London: HMSO, 1905) Chapter XI is devoted to physical training

(91)   For example Board of Education, *Recreation and Physical Fitness for Men and Youths* (Physical Training Series No. 15) (London: HMSO, 1937).

(92)   Contact the Association at 162 Kings Cross Road, London WC1X 9DH.

(93)   See J. Newiss (comp.) *Catalogue of the Carnegie Historical Collection of Books on Physical Education, Sport and Recreation and Health Education Published Before 1946* (2nd edition) (Leeds: City of Leeds and Carnegie College, 1971).

(94)   For details of old books contained within a large number of these libraries see C. W. J. Higson (1967 and 1976) ibid.

(95)   See J. A. Mangan *Athleticism: A Comparative Study of the Emergence and Consolidation of An Educational Ideology*, Ph.D. Thesis, University of Glasgow, 1976 and M. Tozer *Physical Education at Thring's Uppingham*, M.Ed. Thesis, University of Leicester, 1974.

(96)   For a more detailed review of Schoebridge's bibliography see R. W. Cox review in *Physical Education Review*, 11, 2 (Autumn, 1988), pp. 156-158.

Name, Subject, Title Index